MALAWI
in Pictures

Sarah DeCapua

Twenty-First Century Books

Contents

INTRODUCTION 4

THE LAND 8

► Topography. The Shire Valley. Plateaus. Mountains. Natural Resources. Rivers and Lakes. Climate. Flora and Fauna. Environmental Concerns. Cities.

HISTORY AND GOVERNMENT 20

► The Maravi. The Ngoni. The Slave Trade and Missionaries. Effects of the Missions. The Scramble for Africa. Nyasaland Districts Protectorate. Early Resistance to British Rule. African Associations. The Central African Federation. The NAC. Hastings Kamuzu Banda. Independence. Life under Banda. After Banda. Government.

THE PEOPLE 36

► Ethnic Groups. Languages. Migratory Workers. Housing. Health. Education. Clothing.

Website address: www.lernerbook

Twenty-First Century Books
A division of Lerner Publishing Group, Inc.
241 First Avenue North
Minneapolis, MN 55401 U.S.A.

web enhanced @ www.vgsbooks.com

CULTURAL LIFE 46

► Literature. Art. Music and Dance. Religion. Holidays. Sports and Recreation. Food.

THE ECONOMY 56

► Services. Agriculture. Industry. Mining and Manufacturing. Transportation. Energy. Communications and Media. The Future.

FOR MORE INFORMATION

► Timeline 66
► Fast Facts 68
► Currency 68
► Flag 69
► National Anthem 69
► Famous People 70
► Sights to See 72
► Glossary 73
► Selected Bibliography 74
► Further Reading and Websites 76
► Index 78

Library of Congress Cataloging-in-Publication Data

DeCapua, Sarah
    Malawi in pictures / by Sarah DeCapua
        p. cm. – (Visual geography series)
    Includes bibliographical references and index.
    ISBN 978-0-8225-8575-6 (lib. bdg. : alk. paper)
    1. Malawi—Juvenile literature. 2. Malawi—Pictorial works—Juvenile literature. I. Title.
DT3174.D4 2009
    968.97—dc22   2007044783

Manufactured in the United States of America
1 2 3 4 5 6 – BP – 14 13 12 11 10 09

INTRODUCTION

Malawi is a small country in southeastern Africa. Malawi's landscape is one of the most beautiful on the continent. The deep trough called the Great Rift Valley runs the length of the country. Lake Malawi, surrounded by scenic mountains, dominates the eastern portion of the land.

Malawi has some of the most fertile soil in southeastern Africa. But the majority of the nation's people—90 percent of whom live in rural areas—are poor. A history of slave trading, colonization, and corrupt leaders has cast a shadow over the country.

People have lived in Malawi since ancient times. They established independent empires around Lake Malawi. In the 1700s and 1800s, Arab and European slave trading hit some areas of Malawi hard. By 1800 the British and other European powers had begun to exploit the region's resources. In 1891 the British established Nyasaland, which included modern Malawi. Malawians worked for independence from foreign rule, which they won in 1964. When self-rule was declared, the nation changed its name to Malawi. This is the European form of the name Maravi. The Maravi were an African people who migrated into the region in the thirteenth century A.D. The two largest ethnic groups in the country—the Chewa and the Nyanja—are descendants of the original Maravi people.

The lifestyle of the ordinary Malawian has improved little since colonial times. Malawi's first president, Hastings Kamuzu Banda, ruled from 1964 to 1994. Banda adopted some economic styles from the West. His policies emphasized foreign investment and encouraged Malawian farmers to sell their crops to government-approved organizations. In spite of a promising start for the newly independent Malawi, Banda's leadership soon turned to one-party dictatorship, or harsh, absolute rule by one leader.

Banda was appointed president for life in 1967, but his dictatorship began to unravel in 1993. In that year, the worst drought of the century struck Malawi. Malawians were tired of the government that

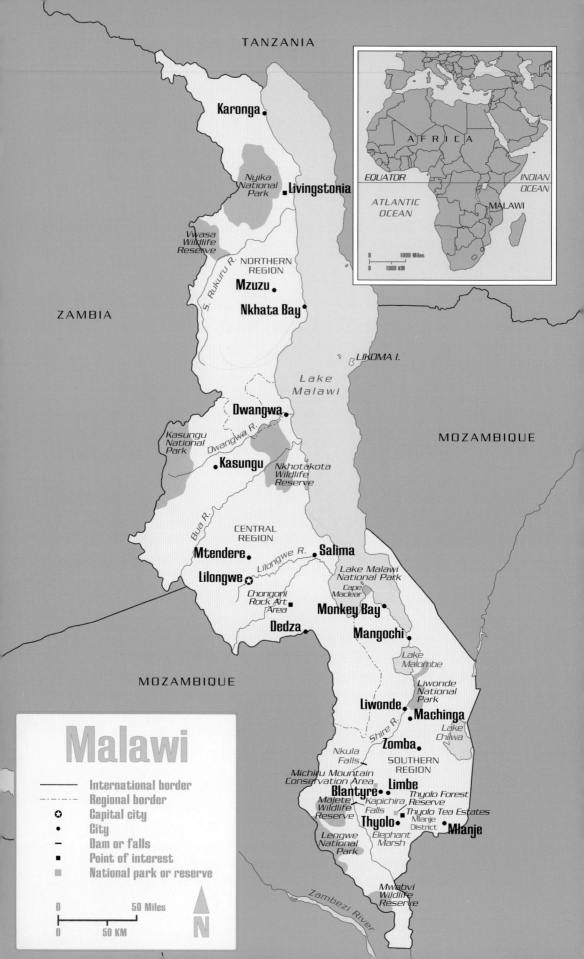

TANZANIA

Karonga

Nyika National Park

Livingstonia

Vwasa Wildlife Reserve

S. Rukuru R.

NORTHERN REGION

Mzuzu

Nkhata Bay

ZAMBIA

Lake Malawi

LIKOMA I.

Dwangwa

Kasungu National Park

Dwangwa R.

Kasungu

Nkhotakota Wildlife Reserve

MOZAMBIQUE

Bua R.

CENTRAL REGION

Mtendere

Lilongwe R.

Salima

Lilongwe

Lake Malawi National Park

Cape Maclear

Chongoni Rock Art Area

Monkey Bay

Dedza

Mangochi

Lake Malombe

MOZAMBIQUE

Liwonde National Park

Liwonde

Machinga

Lake Chilwa

Zomba

Nkula Falls

SOUTHERN REGION

Michiru Mountain Conservation Area

Limbe

Blantyre

Thyolo Forest Reserve

Majete Wildlife Reserve

Kapichira Falls

Thyolo Tea Estates

Mlanje District

Thyolo

Mlanje

Lengwe National Park

Elephant Marsh

Mwabvi Wildlife Reserve

Zambezi River

AFRICA

EQUATOR

ATLANTIC OCEAN

INDIAN OCEAN

MALAWI

0   1000 Miles

0   1000 KM

Malawi

——	International border
–·–·–	Regional border
✪	Capital city
•	City
–	Dam or falls
■	Point of interest
▨	National park or reserve

0   50 Miles

0   50 KM

N

kept them poor. They overwhelmingly voted to end one-party rule in their country.

In 1994 the country held its first free multiparty elections. Citizens elected Bakili Muluzi as president. Muluzi was a successful business-man, so his election made many Malawians hopeful that economic conditions in the country would improve. Muluzi did bring positive change to Malawians, including loosening some of the strict rules that had governed them under Banda. Among the former rules was a national dress code, which forbade women from wearing pants and men from growing their hair long. Muluzi served two terms, but his government didn't bring the permanent economic changes the desperately poor people of this nation were seeking.

After Muluzi, Bingu wa Mutharika won the 2004 presidential election. Foreign observers considered the elections largely unfair. Mutharika began a campaign against government corruption, such as politicians taking bribes. This has led to political conflict that interferes with the country's governance. In spite of conflicts, however, Mutharika has improved the country's health care, infrastructure (public works, such as roads), education, and the economy. But change is slow, and the country faces many challenges.

In 2006 worldwide attention briefly turned to Malawi when a Malawi court gave custody of a Malawian boy named David Banda to U.S. pop singer Madonna and her husband, Guy Ritchie. The story focused media attention on Malawi's challenges. These include lack of education, poverty, inequality between men and women, political tensions, and diseases, especially malaria and the human immunodeficiency virus (HIV).

The worldwide media attention led to a series of fund-raising events in major cities throughout the world. The modern nation of Malawi, with 13.9 million people, isn't asking foreigners to solve their problems, however. They intend to use the aid to meet their challenges themselves. They have a rich history of finding solutions to difficult issues.

Malawi is known as the warm heart of Africa, due to the friendliness of its people. The people look with hope to the future and to claiming their place among the developed countries of the world.

 Visit www.vgsbooks.com for links to websites with additional information about Malawi.

THE LAND

The small southeastern African country of Malawi is wedged among Zambia on the west, Tanzania on the north and east, and Mozambique on the east, south, and west. With no ocean coast, Malawi is a land-locked nation. Long and narrow, the country covers 45,747 square miles (118,485 square kilometers), about the size of the state of Pennsylvania. From north to south, Malawi stretches for 560 miles (900 km). From west to east, its widest span measures 100 miles (160 km). Most of the country is narrow—at some points barely 30 miles (48 km) across.

▶ Topography

The nation is divided into three regions: the Northern, Central, and Southern regions. All are marked by plateaus (raised flatland), hills and mountains, and rivers. The most dominant land feature is a huge rift, or split in the earth. It is part of a much larger formation called the Great Rift Valley. This rift is the result of Earth's crust sinking

millions of years ago. It runs from southwestern Asia to southeastern Africa. The eastern branch of the Great Rift forms a deep valley. It runs the length of Malawi before blending into the plains of Mozambique farther south.

Lake Malawi fills the upper portion of this rift. The lake's northeastern shore forms much of Malawi's border with Tanzania. Part of Malawi's eastern boundary with Mozambique lies within the lake's waters. A series of cliffs and terraces, or flat areas, surround the lake on the Malawian shore.

○ The Shire Valley

Lake Malawi's southern shore has crept northward over thousands of years, uncovering 80 miles (129 km) of the Eastern Rift Valley floor. This area is called the Upper Shire Valley. It is a series of low plains that receive water and silt deposits (bits of soil and sediment) from the Shire River. Foothills and cliffs still mark the original shoreline of the lake.

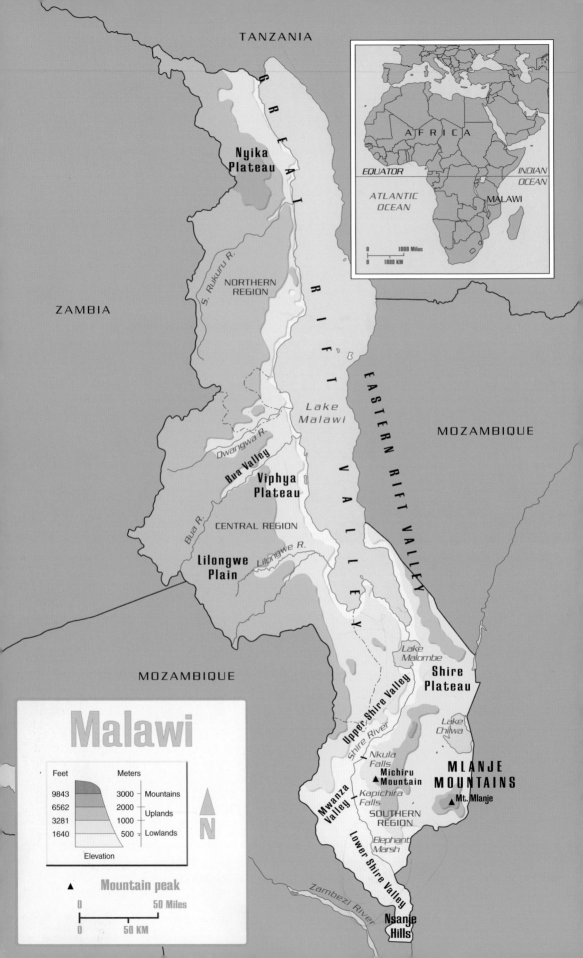

TANZANIA

Nyika
Plateau

ZAMBIA

S. Rukuru R.

NORTHERN
REGION

GREAT

RIFT

Lake
Malawi

EASTERN RIFT VALLEY

MOZAMBIQUE

Dwangwa R.

Bua Valley

Viphya
Plateau

Bua R.

CENTRAL REGION

Lilongwe R.

Lilongwe
Plain

VALLEY

Lake
Malombe

MOZAMBIQUE

Shire
Plateau

Upper Shire Valley

Shire River

Lake
Chilwa

Nkula
Falls

Michiru
Mountain ▲

MLANJE
MOUNTAINS

Kapichira
Falls

Mwanza
Valley

SOUTHERN
REGION

Mt. Mlanje ▲

Lower Shire Valley

Elephant
Marsh

Zambezi River

Nsanje
Hills

Malawi

Feet		Meters	
9843		3000	Mountains
6562		2000	Uplands
3281		1000	
1640		500	Lowlands

Elevation

N

▲ Mountain peak

0 ___ 50 Miles

0 ___ 50 KM

(inset map)

AFRICA

EQUATOR

ATLANTIC
OCEAN

INDIAN
OCEAN

MALAWI

0 ___ 1000 Miles
0 ___ 1000 KM

The Lower Shire Valley occupies the southernmost portion of the channel cut by the Eastern Rift. A smaller valley—the Mwanza—joins the Lower Shire from the west. The valley meets the Nsanje Hills at the southern tip of the country. Despite flooding on the plains and the area's large swamps, farming in the Lower Shire Valley is increasing because of the good soil.

Plateaus

Plateaus (sometimes called plains or highlands) make up about three-fourths of Malawi's land surface. Their fertile, shallow valleys and rolling hills support most of the nation's population. The three major plateaus are the Nyika Plateau in the Northern Region, the Lilongwe Plain in the Central Region, and the Shire Plateau in the Southern Region.

The Nyika Plateau is the highest plain in the country. It stands between 7,000 and 8,000 feet (2,100 and 2,400 meters) above sea level. Although it covers 9,000 square miles (23,300 sq. km), the Nyika region is sparsely populated. It is the least productive of the three major plateaus. Its elevation brings cool temperatures.

Mist rises over the **Nyika Plateau** at sunrise. The plateau is known for its rolling grassland and the wild animals that live there.

The elevation also prevents the area from receiving much of the river-carried silt and minerals that enrich the southern plains.

The Lilongwe Plain of the Central Region is composed of low hills, valleys, and *dambos*—areas of moist soil resting on layers of rock. A line of tall granite peaks runs down from the Northern Region. For the most part, however, elevations range between 2,500 and 4,000 feet (760 and 1,200 m) above sea level.

The Shire Plateau is the most widely cultivated and settled area in Malawi, with an area of 2,800 square miles (7,250 sq. km). Both the original capital city of Zomba and the largest city, Blantyre, are in the western portion of this area. The nearby Shire River provides water for farming and a shipping route.

Mountains

Mountains exist primarily in northern and southern Malawi. Several peaks on the Nyika Plateau reach heights of 8,500 feet (2,590 m). The most impressive range is the Mlanje, in the southernmost portion of the country. Some of the mountains in this range exceed 9,000 feet (2,740 m). The highest summit in Malawi is Mount Mlanje. It reaches 9,855 feet (3,000 m).

The steep sides of Mount Mlanje rise above foothills covered with trees. The mountain has a flat, rocky top with many grassy meadows.

Natural Resources

Malawi's rivers provide water for hydroelectric (water) power. Arable land, or land that is suitable for farming, is also an important resource. Mining for limestone, graphite, and granite is the major mining activity in Malawi. These minerals are used in the construction trades. Gemstones, including agate, amethyst, aquamarine, diamonds, garnets, rubies, and sapphires, have been produced on a small scale. The country has small deposits of asbestos, bauxite, and uranium. Malawi has coal deposits too. However, tight government controls on mining and a lack of skilled labor have slowed the development of these resources.

A large hydroelectric dam was completed on the Shire River above Kapichira Falls in 2005. It harnesses the power of rushing water to provide energy to the cities of Blantyre and Limbe. It was the third hydroelectric dam built on the river.

Rivers and Lakes

As a result of its unusual shape, Malawi possesses an efficient watershed system, a series of slopes that guide a country's rivers to a lake or ocean. From the Northern Region to the Central Region, the South Rukuru, Dwangwa, Bua, and Lilongwe rivers run eastward into Lake Malawi. Lake Malawi and rivers in the Southern Region flow into the Shire River. The Shire deposits silt on the many floodplains of the Southern Region before it runs into the Zambezi River in Mozambique.

At **Chisanga Falls,** the Rukuru River pours out of Malawi and into Zambia.

Livingstonia Beach lies on **Lake Malawi near Salima.** Its mild weather and beautiful scenery make it a popular tourist destination.

Also known as Lake Nyasa, Lake Malawi occupies 12,000 square miles (31,000 sq. km). This is about one-fourth of Malawi's total area. Lake Malawi is the third-largest body of water in Africa, after Lakes Victoria and Tanganyika. It is about 355 miles (571 km) long and 59 miles (95 km) across at its widest point. Its average depth is 2,250 feet (686 m). Cliffs rise to 2,000 feet (610 m) near the shoreline in some areas. More than two hundred species of fish flourish in the lake's waters.

The Shire River begins at Lake Malawi and runs south through Lake Malombe—a shallow, 18-mile-long (29 km) body of water. The river drops at a steep section of rocky hills midway between the Upper and Lower Shire valleys. Where the river crosses the international boundary with Mozambique, Malawi's lowest point is found. Rapids and rough water at this spot make travel hazardous. The Shire passes over the Kapichira Falls (formerly Murchison Rapids) and Nkula Falls before reaching the Lower Shire Valley. Water and valuable silts from the north and west collect in sluggish swamplands, such as Elephant Marsh. This huge wetland is 40 miles (64 km) long and 9 miles (14 km) wide.

Hippopotamuses cool down in the Shire River.

After passing through the lower part of the valley, the Shire River flows into Mozambique's Zambezi River. The Zambezi empties into the Indian Ocean to the east. Apart from some smaller, southeastern streams, which feed into Lake Chilwa and its surrounding marshes, the Shire and its tributaries (branches) drain the entire country.

Climate

Malawi lies in the tropics near the equator (midway between the North Pole and the South Pole). Although the tropics are usually the hottest regions of Earth, Malawi's high altitude keeps the climate pleasantly cool much of the year.

Temperatures at high elevations—the Mlanje Mountains and other uplands at 5,000 to 8,000 feet (1,500 to 2,400 m)—range from daytime highs of 92°F (33°C) to nighttime lows of 32°F (0°C). Midlevel elevations (approximately 3,500 feet [1,070 m] above sea level) record temperatures from 80°F to 90°F (27°C to 32°C) in November and from 40°F to 50°F (4°C to 10°C) in July. The low areas of the Shire Valley and some locations near Lake Malawi are the hottest and most humid in the country. Only about 200 feet (61 m)

Malawi's location in the Southern Hemisphere means its seasons are opposite of those in the Northern Hemisphere. Winter occurs from June to September. The summer months are December through March.

above sea level, these areas have an average temperature of 89°F (32°C). Sometimes temperatures climb above 100°F (38°C). Humidity at this elevation hovers at about 80 percent throughout the year. The high moisture content makes the warm air feel heavy and sticky.

Little rain falls from May to October. In the one long rainy season from November to April, rainfall varies. The Shire River valley and the shores of Lake Malawi receive 25 to 35 inches (64 to 89 centimeters) of rain a year. The highlands receive between 100 and 130 inches (254 and 330 cm) of rain a year.

Flora and Fauna

Savanna woodlands—a mixture of scrub plants, thorn bushes, coarse grasses, and widely scattered trees—cover most of Malawi. Dense forests replace the savanna only in wet areas, such as Nkhata Bay, the northern part of the Nsanje Hills, and the Mlanje Mountains to the south. These forests are a mixture of evergreen and deciduous (leaf-shedding) trees. Baobab trees dot the landscape. They are marked by twisted branches and thick, gray, barkless trunks. At lower altitudes, mahogany, ebony, teak, and palm trees are common.

Also in the lowlands—or in wet areas such as dambos—marsh grasses, sedge, and reeds abound. These plants provide grazing for cattle and wildlife during the dry months when the savanna is bare of plants. Some families have cleared dambos and marshes to make small farm plots.

Malawi is home to 192 species of mammals. On the plateaus, leopards, bushbuck, wild pigs, vervet monkeys, and baboons roam freely. Other mammals include porcupines, civets, servals, bush babies, and waterbuck. Lions, zebras, cheetahs, buffalo, elephants, and many species of antelope are also found in Malawi.

There are 664 kinds of birds in Malawi. Some of Malawi's birds cannot be found anywhere else in Africa. Familiar species

A stand of **baobab trees** grows near Mangochi. The trees produce edible leaves and fruit.

Malawi's **chacma baboon (left)** is one of the largest kinds of baboon. The **Boehm's bee-eater (right)** is famous for catching bees and hitting them against rocks to remove their stingers before eating them.

include the sparrow and the owl. More exotic varieties are fish eagles, Denham's bustards, wattled cranes, cormorants, weaverbirds, and red-winged francolins.

More than four hundred species of fish swim in Malawi's waters, including *mpasa*, or lake salmon. Also in the waters are crocodiles, water moccasin snakes, and otters. Elephants and hippopotamuses live in Lake Malawi.

Aside from crocodiles, common reptiles include the tortoise and poisonous snakes such as the hooded cobra. Mosquitoes and other disease-carrying insects present a serious health hazard. Tsetse flies carry the virus that causes sleeping sickness. This illness threatens people and livestock in much of the nation.

Many kinds of spiders and insects are found in Malawi. Spiders include baboon spiders, which are members of the tarantula family, and straight horn spiders. Insects include grasshoppers, caterpillars, and white ants (termites).

Malawi's government has set up many game parks and preserves to protect wildlife and to provide a means of viewing the animals in

Malawi has no national bird, but many Malawians' favorite bird is the bar-tailed trogon. About 1 foot tall (30 cm), this brilliantly colored bird lives in the forest. Its head and throat are covered in emerald green feathers. Its bill is yellow. Red feathers cover its chest and belly. Its tail contains silver feathers with black stripes. The bird was named for its striped tail feathers. It lives in holes in trees and eats insects.

MICHIRU MOUNTAIN CONSERVATION AREA

Overlooking Blantyre is the Michiru Mountain Conservation Area. The site is actually an ongoing experiment in conservation. Experts there demonstrate wise land use. The area is divided into three sections: a forestry reserve, a farming area, and a nature reserve for the preservation of natural resources. Visitors to the area can drive to the summit of Michiru Mountain to enjoy spectacular views of Blantyre and the Shire Valley.

their natural habitats. More than 3,000 square miles (7,800 sq. km) of the country have been set aside as national parks and preserves.

○ Environmental Concerns

Malawi's environmental issues include desertification and deforestation. Desertification is the process of land becoming desert. It occurs when land is misused by humans or overgrazed by livestock. Nothing will grow on the resulting drylands. Deforestation occurs when woodlands are lost to human development. People cut down trees for building material and fuel. When trees are cut down faster than they can be replaced, soil erosion occurs. Erosion is the carrying away of soil, rock, and sediment by wind and water.

Water shortages also affect life in Malawi. The country has periods of severe drought (lack of rainfall). Plants die, and people and animals struggle to find food. Lack of potable (clean drinking) water also affects Malawians. Rural dwellers must walk, sometimes several miles, to wells, rivers, or water donation stations. Water from wells, rivers, or even from damaged water pipes may contain disease-causing insects, bacteria, or parasites.

Water pollution from farming and industrial chemicals is another environmental issue facing Malawi. The proper disposal of sewage is a problem in rural areas and in shantytowns on the outskirts of cities. The Malawi government seeks ways to help citizens solve these issues.

○ Cities

Only 10 percent of Malawi's people live in urban areas. The southern third of the country contains more than half of the total population because of the richness of the soil. Most Malawians are farmers.

Visit www.vgsbooks.com for links to websites with additional information about Malawi's geography, wild animals, and cities.

Workers drive down a street in **Lilongwe's Old Town.** Lilongwe is the capital of Malawi.

BLANTYRE, Malawi's largest city, covers 83 square miles (215 sq. km) in the Southern Region. It includes the two communities of Blantyre and Limbe, which are 5 miles (8 km) apart. Together they have a population of more than five hundred thousand. Blantyre is the country's main commercial, industrial, and communications hub. It is also home to Malawi's National Museum. Mandala House, built in 1882, is the oldest building in Malawi. It is also in Blantyre. Upper- and middle-class housing is like that found in prosperous cities throughout the world. People with less money live in traditional Malawian round houses with thatched grass roofs. Slum dwellings of cardboard and tin also exist.

LILONGWE is the capital of Malawi. The city took more than ten years to build and cost more than $15 million. Loans from the Republic of South Africa helped to build the city in the 1970s. In 1975 Lilongwe replaced Zomba as the nation's capital. With a population of more than six hundred thousand, Lilongwe lies between 3,400 and 3,600 feet (1,040 m and 1,100 m) above sea level. Because of the altitude, the climate is fairly mild. The temperature varies from an average of 74°F (23°C) in the winter to 86°F (30°C) in the summer. The capital's population has boomed since its early days. This has resulted in crowded streets and poor-quality housing.

ZOMBA is about 60 miles (97 km) northeast of Blantyre, on the Shire Plateau. Zomba is the country's third-largest city (population 100,000) and a center for light industry and agricultural trade. Many old structures remain as reminders of the period when Malawi was a British colony. The State House and Old Residency stand beside modern medical and educational buildings. The main campus of the University of Malawi and the National Archives of Malawi are both located in Zomba.

HISTORY AND GOVERNMENT

Human beings have lived in the area that became Malawi since pre-historic times. Anthropologists believe that the ancestors of modern humans lived in southern Africa about two million years ago. Scientists have found the remains of human settlements dating back about one hundred thousand years along the shores of Lake Malawi. Archaeologists believe these people were the ancestors of some of the peoples of central Africa and the San (Bushmen) of southern Africa. They hunted large animals, including elephants, with simple stone tools.

About five thousand years ago, the Katanga and Kafula people lived in the Lake Malawi region. They, too, hunted with stone tools. They also gathered plants for food. Rock paintings at present-day Chongoni Rock Art Area near Dedza are evidence of their existence.

About two thousand years ago, the Yao and other Bantu-speaking peoples moved into northern Malawi from modern-day Tanzania. They were skilled ironworkers and farmers. Well-made tools have been found that provide clues about their lives.

In the A.D. 700s, Arab slave traders arrived in the area. Slave trading had existed in Africa for thousands of years. However, after slave traders arrived in what became Malawi, slave trading increased. The present-day cities of Nkhotakota and Karonga served as slave trade centers. Africans were among the groups Arab traders sent by ship to the Middle East by way of Madagascar (an island off the southeast coast of Africa). Once the Africans arrived in the Middle East, they were sold as slaves.

The Maravi

The Maravi were the first large group of people to enter the area around Lake Malawi. Their leader, Mazizi, led them there from the Congo River basin. They established the Maravi Empire about 1480, with Mazizi as their *karonga* (king). After Mazizi's death, the group split into several smaller units. By the sixteenth century, Maravi states (systems of centralized government) dominated the southern and western regions, including the Shire River valley.

A LAND OF KINGDOMS

Established in 1480, the Maravi Empire existed for nearly two hundred years. During the 1500s, the empire included most of modern-day central and southern Malawi. At the height of its power in the 1600s, the empire influenced people as far away as modern Zambia and Mozambique.

North of the Maravi territory, people known as the Ngonde founded a kingdom about 1600. In the 1700s, people from present-day Mozambique moved into the area around Lake Malawi. They established the Chikulamayembe Kingdom south of the Ngonde Kingdom.

Two groups—the Katanga and the Kafula—already occupied the area to the southwest of the lake. The Katanga were peaceful people and were easily absorbed by the Maravi. The nomadic (migratory) Kafula fought the Maravi with iron-tipped darts that were coated with poison. Eventually, however, the Maravi drove the Kafula into what became the nations of Zambia and Mozambique.

Also in the sixteenth century, explorers from Portugal became the first Europeans to arrive in what became Malawi. They reached the area in the 1500s from the east coast of Mozambique. They were seeking a water route to central Africa.

The ruling Maravi leader granted the land west of Lake Malawi to two smaller Maravi communities. Together they became known as the Chewa. By the end of the sixteenth century, the Chewa and other Maravi peoples had developed long-distance trade contacts with Kilwa. Kilwa was a coastal trading center located in present-day Tanzania. They traded ivory elephant tusks and slaves with traders from the Middle East and beyond. The Portuguese began to take away the Maravi's traditional trade in ivory.

The Portuguese were not the only Europeans looking to Africa for increased trade, power, and fame. In the 1700s, Great Britain experienced the beginnings of the Industrial Revolution. The Industrial Revolution was a period when countries shifted their economies from agriculture to manufacturing. Soon Great Britain and other European powers, including France and Portugal, sought to gain raw materials for their expanding industries. They looked to the continent of Africa for its wood and metals. They sent explorers to map the continent and to determine the extent of its resources. They also made huge profits in the slave trade. Until the beginning of the nineteenth century, the slave trade in Malawi had existed mostly among local groups. Warriors captured in battle were kept or sold to villages. On rare occasions, a Portuguese ship would raid the Lower Shire valley and carry away Africans as slaves.

The Maravi reunited under a single leader. They reached the height of their power in the seventeenth century. But by the 1800s, they were vying for goods against growing numbers of competitors such as the Portuguese. The Swahili—a people of mixed African and Arab descent—posed additional competition. They ran slaves and goods from their villages on the east coast of Africa to the island of Zanzibar, in the Indian Ocean.

Loss of trade, combined with the long distances between the various groups and their main ruler, weakened the central authority of the Maravi Empire. By 1800 powerful local leaders were bargaining with the Portuguese for weapons. Soon the local groups were fully independent of their ties to the empire.

The Ngoni

In the early 1800s, refugees began to migrate northward from southern Africa. They were escaping the forces of Shaka, the Zulu leader who was taking over lands and peoples in southern Africa. In 1835 one of these refugee groups, the Jere Ngoni, crossed the Zambezi River and moved north into Malawi. Under their leader, Zwangendaba, the Jere Ngoni conquered and absorbed the peoples they met on their journey.

The Maseko Ngoni, a related group that also moved north to escape the Zulu, circled Lake Malawi before settling west of the lake. The stronger Maseko Ngoni absorbed the Chewa. Their combined armies drove out the warlike Yao, who were the area's most active slave traders. Although the Ngoni ruled, they adopted the language of the more numerous Chewa.

The Slave Trade and Missionaries

Due to public outcry in Great Britain against the cruelties of slavery, the nineteenth-century British government was committed to ending the African slave trade. In 1817 Radama I, the king of Madagascar, signed an agreement with the British government. They agreed to slow Madagascar's slave trade. This significantly cut the flow of slaves from the east coast to the Middle East. As a result, coastal slave traders, principally the Yao, moved toward the African interior, where they captured many Maravi. The captives were made to walk in long slave caravans, or traveling groups, to ships on the east coast.

Radama I

The westward movement of the slave traders was slowed when the Maseko Ngoni moved into the Lilongwe Plain and the Lake Malawi area about 1860. Unlike the splintered Maravi, this Ngoni group had an excellent military organization. The Yao peoples lacked the slaves they needed to exchange for weapons, so they began to supply slaves from their own population.

European missionaries (religious teachers) also traveled to Africa in the 1800s. They sought to spread their Christian religion and European ways. Missionaries tried to end slavery, which was against their beliefs. However, they also tried to make local people give up their ancient religious traditions.

A Scottish missionary and explorer, David Livingstone (1813–1873), reached the Lake Malawi region in the mid-nineteenth century. Livingstone opposed the slave trade. He searched for a trade route that would be profitable enough to replace the slave trade. He also believed that the new traders in the region would fund Christian missions, or church and school settlements, throughout the African interior.

Between 1858 and 1863, Livingstone ventured into the area four times. He mapped the Shire River valley and Lake Malawi (which he called Lake Nyasa) for the first time in 1859. Largely as a result of the explorer's influence, committees from four universities in Great Britain established the Universities Mission to Central Africa (UMCA).

At this stage, the British government was more interested in temporary, profitable trade than in acquiring colonies. Colonies were expensive and hard to maintain.

LIVINGSTONE HONORED

Throughout Africa a variety of place-names and honors commemorate explorer David Livingstone. In Malawi the mission settlement of Livingstonia dates to 1894. Blantyre is named for Livingstone's birthplace in Lanarkshire, Scotland, and includes a memorial to him. In addition, the David Livingstone Scholarships are awarded to students at the University of Malawi.

In this 1867 portrait, David Livingstone holds a map of Africa.

Yao people listen to **a lesson on Christianity at a mission school.** This village later became the city of Mangochi, Malawi.

Livingstone's search for a faster trade route fit the economic plans of the British government. It also gave him money for his expeditions (journeys). Later, Great Britain used Livingstone's discoveries and influence to claim African territory.

In 1858 Livingstone was sent to Quelimane, in modern-day Mozambique, as a representative of the British government. Livingstone's orders were to make contact with local African leaders. He set up the first mission in the Shire Plateau in 1861, which made Malawi a center for Christian missionary activity in southeastern Africa.

Effects of the Missions

The missions developed their own economies and expanded rapidly, even after Livingstone's death in 1873. For example, more than 35,000 acres (14,000 hectares) of coffee were grown at the Zambezi Industrial Mission. By 1885 Livingstonia missions (missions David Livingstone established) had thirty-five schools in operation. At these schools, Africans learned trades—some of which they were already quite skilled in—such as carpentry and agriculture. Missionaries also taught Christianity and the English language. Although the missionaries were well meaning, they knew little of the land and culture of the peoples among whom they lived.

The desire to spread Christianity and the desire to exploit the wealth of Africa were sometimes hard to tell apart. Missionaries wanted to halt the slave trade for humanitarian reasons. European businesspeople wanted to stop the trade because it was taking away both customers for their imported goods and labor for their plantations (large farms). The people of the area had a more personal stake in ending the trade: keeping their families intact.

Slowly, local ethnic groups lost their trade customers to Europeans. The traditional role of ethnic groups of the interior—to carry goods to and from the coast—had often rested on their ability to pass safely through hostile territory. But the Europeans built new rail lines and ran armed steamships on Lake Malawi. So they were able to move large amounts of goods safely and more quickly.

Livingstone's exploration of the Shire River actually led to an increase in the slave trade. Swahili and Portuguese traders gained a way to move oceangoing ships into the Upper Shire valley.

The Scramble for Africa

The presence of the British in the Malawi area aroused the interest of other Western powers. They worried they might get only a small portion of valuable African lands. Although the British, French, and Portuguese had been exploring Africa and claiming various parts of it, most of the continent was still unmapped. In the 1880s, however, Belgium and Germany came on the scene, and soon a rush—often called the Scramble for Africa—began. European countries hurried to stake claims and to establish control over huge areas they had not yet explored.

The following decade saw increased European expansion into Africa. Usually European governments could claim lands only if the leaders of local groups signed treaties allowing the claims. Local leaders were offered yearly payments, protection by the foreign government, and weapons in exchange for signing the treaties.

Local people watch as **an explorer claims a stretch of the Shire River** as British property by raising the British flag on its shore.

Though the British government promised to take land only by treaty, it fought the Chewa, the Maseko Ngoni, and the Yao. The British signed treaties with these peoples after defeating them in battle. In spite of European promises to protect rather than to take over territory, local ethnic influence was lost.

Geography, as well as European treaties, determined the shape of the colony that would become independent Malawi. Lake Malawi formed the region's eastern border, and British treaties or land grants determined all other borders. In dividing up the African continent, the Europeans established boundaries that separated traditional communities. Many ethnic groups were split among British, Portuguese, and French rulers. In the region of Nyasaland, this situation prevented the people from having a powerful voice in their country's affairs.

Nyasaland Districts Protectorate

In 1891 Britain proclaimed a protectorate—called the Nyasaland Districts Protectorate—over the large area north of the Zambezi River. A protectorate is a region under the control of a more powerful foreign government. The more powerful government is called the protector. Protectors intend to provide military or diplomatic defense to the protectorate. Often, however, the protector exploits the protectorate's land, resources, and people. The Nyasaland Districts Protectorate included areas of present-day Malawi, Zimbabwe, and Zambia. The British government appointed Sir Harry Johnston as head of the protectorate.

One of Johnston's first tasks was to end the slave trade and to impose British rule at the southern end of Lake Malawi. There Yao slave traders still raided the countryside. He built Fort Johnston (modern Mangochi) as a southern base and freed 270 slaves

Sir Harry Johnston made many trips through Africa, including an expedition to study Tanzania's Mount Kilimanjaro.

who were about to be sent to the coast. The Yao leaders responded by intensifying their raids.

Additional British forces arrived from Cape Town, South Africa. With them Johnston attacked the fighters of the Yao leader, Makanjira. Although Makanjira's village was destroyed twice, he escaped to Portuguese territory. The British defeated the Yao slave traders in December 1895. The British then took control of Nyasaland.

> Makanjira continually frustrated Johnston's efforts to end the slave trade. Makanjira obtained guns from Arab traders and trained his Yao fighters in European-style warfare. He repeatedly stole boats from the Universities Mission headquarters for use in the slave trade. Eventually the Yao were defeated, but Makanjira escaped from the British.

After ending the slave trade in Nyasaland, Harry Johnston set up a British-style government there. He divided the country into districts and put each one under the control of an official, or magistrate. In addition, he brought in tax collectors, an accountant, a medical officer, and a group of surveyors who marked boundaries and laid out roads. Johnston chose Zomba as the capital and built a large home there.

Some Africans could not pay the taxes the British imposed on them, so they moved into surrounding countries, including what later became Zimbabwe, Zambia, and South Africa. There they worked on farms and in mines. They sent the money they earned to their families in Nyasaland, who used it to pay the taxes.

◉ Early Resistance to British Rule

In 1907 the British renamed the territory the Nyasaland Protectorate. They established lawmaking bodies, which did not allow African members. Only one missionary was permitted to speak for the Africans.

The small number of European-educated Africans in Nyasaland worked mostly as guides on trips because they knew their land. They also worked as language interpreters between locals and the British. There were exceptions, however. John Chilembwe, a Yao, studied in both Nyasaland and the United States. One of Chilembwe's early influences in Nyasaland was Joseph Booth. Booth was a British missionary and founder of the Zambezi Industrial Mission. The British forced Booth to leave Nyasaland because he spoke out in support of African nationalism, or self-rule. African nationalism called for Africans, not Europeans, to control Africa.

In 1900 Chilembwe established a number of schools in Nyasaland. He also became head of an independent African church in the Southern Region. He began to demand equal opportunities for Africans.

The colonial government moved slowly to improve everyday life for Africans. Chilembwe thought a show of force—even a weak show of force—was necessary to convince the British to work faster to improve Africans' lives. Chilembwe and a small number of followers staged what came to be called the Chilembwe Rising of 1915. During the revolt, Chilembwe was killed by British troops, who quickly ended the rebellion. Chilembwe's effort, however, helped to form a new national identity by breaking down the traditional barriers among Nyasaland's ethnic groups. Chilembwe is remembered as the first African in Nyasaland to die protesting British rule.

Joseph Booth (1851–1932) was a British missionary in what became modern-day Malawi, Lesotho, and South Africa. In 1897 Booth wrote the book *Africa for the Africans*, becoming the first known European to use the phrase. He popularized Africans' rejection of colonialism and their demands for education, political participation, and justice equal to that of whites. His book helped people outside Africa to understand the desire of Africans to be free of colonial rule.

African Associations

In addition to Chilembwe's movement, a number of other African political associations also developed in the early twentieth century. They were called Native Associations. The membership of these organizations was primarily mission educated and included all ethnic groups. The first Native Association was established in 1912 at Karonga. Between 1912 and the 1930s, nine other groups formed. These groups worked for government representation and better working conditions for Africans.

In October 1944, the Nyasaland African Congress (NAC) became the colony's first nationwide African organization. Seventeen ethnic associations joined the NAC. But members soon accused the NAC of dishonest management and of favoring certain ethnic groups. The association lost the popular support (support of the people) it had been building. The weakened NAC was unable to protest effectively against the British government's plan to federate (combine) the colonies of Northern Rhodesia, Southern Rhodesia, and Nyasaland—the modern nations of Zambia, Zimbabwe, and Malawi.

Farm laborers bring baskets of harvested tea leaves to be weighed in **Nyasaland in the 1950s.** European settlers hired Africans to work on large farms in Nyasaland and Southern Rhodesia.

The Central African Federation

European settlers in Southern Rhodesia wanted the British government to federate the three colonies. Federation would strengthen the colonies' economies. In addition, many European settlers had come to regard Africa as their permanent home. Nyasaland settlers thought that joining with Southern Rhodesia—and its large white population—would provide economic benefits.

Soon a campaign by Africans to resist federation began in Nyasaland. Most local groups believed the change would make them lose their ethnic identities. Despite African protests, the British formed the Central African Federation on August 1, 1953.

Many ethnic groups in Nyasaland had not wanted to work together in the past because of their ethnic differences. But they all agreed that they didn't want the new federation. In this way, the British government's actions actually helped create African unity. Groups in rural villages and in cities organized to oppose the federation.

The NAC

The federation issue helped the NAC regain popular support and grow stronger. By April 1957, it had more than sixty thousand members. Two new leaders of the NAC—Henry B. M. Chipembere and Kanyama Chiume—were responsible for much of this growth. Both men had studied outside of Nyasaland. They returned to aid the struggle against federation.

The NAC developed the symbols of a political party—a slogan of *Kwaca* (the dawn), a national flag, and a weekly newsletter. The NAC also glorified the activities of John Chilembwe. The party, however, still lacked an experienced leader with popular appeal. The party turned to Hastings Kamuzu Banda.

Hastings Kamuzu Banda

Throughout Nyasaland's colonization by the British, Hastings Banda watched the political developments from abroad. Born in the Kasungu area of Nyasaland around 1906, Banda was mission educated. After holding several jobs in South Africa and Southern Rhodesia, he came to the attention of a group of U.S. missionaries. They sent him to the United States, where he attended high school and college and where he became a physician in 1937.

Banda stayed in Great Britain during World War II (1939–1945) and soon had a thriving medical practice in London. His home became the meeting place of Africans who lived in Great Britain, and he became involved in African politics. In 1958 Banda returned to his homeland. At that time, the young leadership of the NAC invited him to become the head of their organization. The NAC leaders hoped to use Banda's professional image and experience to unite the people.

Banda was so successful in gaining local support that just one year after he was invited to head the NAC, British authorities arrested him. The British also passed laws to keep Africans from meeting in large groups. British authorities thought keeping people from gathering would loosen support for Banda.

Cheering supporters surround **Hastings Banda** shortly after his return to Malawi in 1958.

Although the NAC used nonviolent methods when it began, disturbances, rioting, and violence became frequent in the 1950s. The British banned the NAC. Banda's supporters formed the Malawi Congress Party (MCP) to take its place. Faced with increased governmental restrictions, African opposition to the British grew. To ease the tension, the British released Banda from jail in 1961 and invited him to London for a constitutional conference. Great Britain had seen that the tide was turning toward independence for Nyasaland. The conference was held to write a constitution (document that outlines governing laws) for Nyasaland. It was a step toward independence for the colony. The constitution gave the Africans of Nyasaland the right to vote. After the conference, elections were held in Nyasaland. Banda's MCP won by an overwhelming majority.

Independence

After the 1961 elections, Great Britain was finally willing to withdraw from Nyasaland. But first, Nyasaland politicians had to show that they were capable of self-government. During 1961 and 1962, the people of Nyasaland showed their ability to manage their own affairs. The MCP then took full control of the country's government. A new constitution was agreed upon, and Nyasaland became the independent republic of Malawi on July 6, 1964. Its first president was Hastings Kamuzu Banda.

Banda's presidency quickly became a dictatorship. He refused to allow the members of his cabinet (advisers) to speak their minds. When six cabinet members demanded that Malawi support other colonies of Africans that were fighting for independence, Banda forced them to resign. Banda formed a police force and army that harassed those who disagreed with his policies.

An unsuccessful revolt, led by one of Banda's opponents from the Yao ethnic group, broke out in 1965. Two years later, a former cabinet member organized another attack against Banda's government. The unstable situation led Malawi's Parliament (lawmaking body) to name Banda president for life.

Life under Banda

As president, Banda once said, "One leader, one party, one government, and no nonsense about it." He required that all Malawians belong to the MCP. He established units of secret police and a militia (armed group) called Young Pioneers of the MCP. The Young Pioneers was made up of Malawian youths who received military-style training in remote locations of the country. They were reportedly responsible for the murder of hundreds of Malawians suspected of opposing Banda's rule.

Although Malawi's constitution guaranteed civil rights, Banda largely ignored them. Malawians were often arrested without charge and jailed without trial. Banda's government also passed laws that required every business to have an official portrait of him hanging on the wall. No poster, clock, or picture could be higher than his picture. Churches had to be government approved. The government also tightly controlled the press and radio, which served mainly as outlets for government propaganda. Television was banned.

The government closely supervised Malawians' personal lives as well. Banda even made a dress code. Women were not allowed to wear pants, and the hemlines of skirts or dresses had to fall below the knees. It was unlawful for men to have long hair or beards. Government agents opened and often edited mail. They tapped telephones to catch anyone who might be speaking against the government. (Speaking out against Banda's government was punishable by arrest, exile from the country, and sometimes death.)

However, Banda supported women's rights. He formed an organization to address the concerns, needs, rights, and opportunities of women in Malawi. He also improved the country's infrastructure, which included the establishment of major roads, airports, hospitals, and schools. He founded Kamuzu Academy, where Malawian children were taught the Latin and ancient Greek languages, like upper-class British children of the era.

After Banda

In 1992 Malawi suffered the worst drought of the twentieth century. That same year, violent protests against Banda's rule began. Western nations suspended aid to the country to show their opposition to Banda. In a 1993 referendum (vote), Malawians voted overwhelmingly for an end to one-party rule. Parliament passed laws establishing a multiparty democracy and abolishing the life presidency.

In a free election in 1994, Banda was defeated by Bakili Muluzi. Muluzi was a former member of Banda's government

"YOUR EXCELLENCY"

The government of newly elected president Bakili Muluzi charged Hastings Banda for crimes committed against humanity during Banda's rule. The charges included murder for the 1983 deaths of three of Banda's cabinet members, as well as a member of Parliament.

Banda was acquitted (found not guilty) at his trial and spent the remainder of his life in South Africa. He lived quietly, surrounded by servants who called him "Your Excellency." Banda never married or had children. He always kept his exact age a secret and may have been as old as 101 when he died in 1997.

Bakili Muluzi

and the founder of the United Democratic Front (UDF) political party. Muluzi's presidency brought greater democracy to Malawi. He freed prisoners arrested by Banda and reestablished freedom of speech and assembly. Muluzi aimed to end government corruption that was marked by officials receiving bribes and employing family members. He also promised to reduce poverty and food shortages in the country. Muluzi was reelected in 1999. However, his opponent challenged the election results. The aftermath of the election included demonstrations, violence, and widespread looting (stealing). During Muluzi's second term, Malawians and foreign observers criticized him for being increasingly dictatorial.

In 2000 the country drew international praise when its small air force aided nearly one thousand flood victims in neighboring Mozambique. By 2002, however, another drought in Malawi had led to severe food shortages. The government struggled to obtain food for hungry Malawians.

The constitution limited Muluzi to two terms in office. He tried to change the constitution to continue his presidency but was unsuccessful. In 2004 Bingu wa Mutharika—the UDF candidate—was elected president. Many foreign observers claim the election was unfair because of voting irregularities. For example, in some villages voters cast more than one vote. Regardless of rumored election problems, Mutharika took over the government. He launched an anticorruption campaign that angered many in his party. As a result, in 2005 Mutharika left the UDF and established the Democratic Progressive Party (DPP). A crop failure that same year resulted in further food shortages and high food prices. The UDF blamed Mutharika. The party tried but failed to have him impeached (removed from office). In his 2007 New Year's message, President Mutharika accused the country's opposition parties of dividing the nation but vowed to seek reelection in 2009.

Also in 2007, international pop star Madonna made a documentary (nonfiction) film about the challenges facing Malawians. The film is called *I Am Because We Are*. It was released at the Tribeca Film Festival in New York City in 2008.

◉ Government

Malawi has been a multiparty democracy since 1994. Under the 1995 constitution, the president, who is both chief of state and head of the government, is chosen through national direct election. One term of office lasts five years, with a two-term limit. A vice president is elected

Malawi's lawmakers meet in Zomba.

with the president. The president may appoint a second vice president, who must be from a different party. The fourteen members of the president's cabinet can be drawn from within or outside the legislature.

Since 1994 the legislature, which had been called Parliament, has been known as the National Assembly. The National Assembly, Malawi's lawmaking body, has 193 seats. All members are directly elected by the people and serve five-year terms. The constitution provides for a second, eighty-member house called a senate. As of 2008, the senate had not yet been created. In an effort to recognize the right of Malawian women to participate in government, seventeen women hold government positions, including in the legislature and cabinet.

Malawi's judicial system is made up of lower courts, a high court, a Supreme Court of Appeals, and a constitutional court. The president appoints the chief justice, or head of the Supreme Court of Appeals. The Judicial Service Commission nominates judges for lower courts. The president must approve those nominations.

Local government is divided into three regions that are headed by regional administrators. Those three regions are further divided into twenty-four districts, headed by district commissioners. District councils, elected by citizens of the districts, are in charge of a variety of services. Among them are postal services, roads, and water supplies. District councils are also responsible for providing primary education. Some councils also run public health clinics.

Visit www.vgsbooks.com for links to websites with additional information about the history and government of Malawi, including links to the web pages of Malawi's president and National Assembly.

THE PEOPLE

About 90 percent of Malawi's 13.9 million people live in rural villages. The population is distributed unevenly. More than half the population live in the Southern Region, where two of Malawi's three largest cities—Blantyre and Zomba—are located. The Northern Region has only about 10 percent of the people. The Central Region has 40 percent.

Malawi has more people per square mile than any other country in southeastern Africa. The nation averages 384 people per square mile (148 per sq. km). Compare this with neighboring Zambia, where there are 41 people per square mile (16 per sq. km), and with Mozambique, where there are 70 people per square mile (27 per sq. km). Malawi's population growth rate is 2.3 percent, a similar rate of growth for much of Africa. Population growth has slowed since the 1980s as a result of the high rate of HIV/AIDS in Malawi. The average woman in Malawi will give birth six times in her lifetime. Experts expect the population to reach 20 million by 2025.

Ethnic Groups

Malawi's people are 99 percent African and belong to several different ethnic groups. A variety of ethnic groups—including the Tonga and the Sena—have lived in Malawi only since the late 1800s, when their migrations brought them to the area. The Banda government discouraged ethnic loyalties in order to promote national loyalty. Consequently, the nation's people became less conscious of their regional traditions. Since the end of the Banda regime, Malawians have again embraced ethnic traditions.

The Chewa and Nyanja are both descended from the Maravi who migrated to present-day Malawi in the thirteenth century. Together they make up about 60 percent of the population. Both groups speak Chichewa, a language originally called Chinyanja, after the Nyanja people. The government changed the name when the first census (population count) after independence showed that the Chewa were the largest group speaking Chinyanja.

Children play with tires in a village outside Lilongwe.

The Chewa dominate Lilongwe, Dedza, Nkhotakota, and other areas of the Central Region. *Nyanja* means "people of the lake." This group outnumbers other groups of the Southern Region, which includes Lake Chilwa and the southern shore of Lake Malawi. Occupying the eastern part of the Southern Region, the Lomwe represent 15 percent of Malawi's population. Many of the Lomwe in Malawi are migrant workers from Mozambique who come seasonally in search of employment on the tea or cotton estates. Many of these people have settled into a life of rice cultivation in Malawi.

The Yao, Ngoni, Tumbuka, Tonga, Sena, and Ngonde together form about 24 percent of the population. Figures for the Tonga and Yao are difficult to verify because, like the Lomwe, they travel outside the country in search of better jobs. Many Yao are employed in Zimbabwe's mines or in Zambia's agricultural industries.

Europeans and Asians also live in Malawi. Most Europeans are British

THE NYANJA

The Nyanja people (also called Mang'anja) speak Chichewa, a language spoken in other places in central and southern Africa. Significant numbers of Nyanja people are found in the neighboring countries of Zambia, Zimbabwe, Mozambique, and Tanzania.

and Portuguese from Mozambique. Asians are mostly Indians, Koreans, and Lebanese. Together, Europeans and Asians make up about 1 percent of Malawi's population.

Languages

English and Chichewa are the official languages of Malawi. English became the national language in 1968, but everyday interactions are conducted mostly in Chichewa. Students in elementary school are taught both English and Chichewa. Malawians also speak a variety of other Bantu-related languages, including Chitumbuka and Chiyao. The prefix *chi-* means "the language of." So *Chichewa* means "the language of the Chewa tribe." *Chitumbuka* means "the language of the Tumbuka tribe." *Chiyao* means "the language of the Yao tribe." Other tribal languages spoken in Malawi include Chitonga, Chisena, and Chingonde.

WHAT'S IN A NAME?

The most popular Chichewa names for Malawian girls are Mesi, which means "water," and Chimwala, which means "stone." Popular Chichewa names for Malawian boys are Azibo (earth) and Bomani (warrior). Children receive English names as well. The most common are Gracious, Happiness, Brightness, and Rejoice. One of the most popular is Last. These names are given to both boys and girls.

Migratory Workers

In the colonial era, Malawian workers moved into surrounding countries to earn money to pay British taxes. Since then migratory workers have continued to participate in the cash economies of other countries, which allows them to send money back to their families or to purchase consumer goods.

Malawian migrant workers traditionally have labored in the mines and fields of Zimbabwe, Zambia, and South Africa. About 60 percent of all Malawian men have worked outside the country at least once.

Although gone for long periods of time, the majority of workers continue to participate in family decisions by mail. When male migrants return, they reclaim their place as the heads of their families. For

In the mid-1970s, more than three hundred thousand Malawians had left the country to find work. Thirty years later, in the early 2000s, that number had more than doubled to seven hundred thousand.

some ethnic groups, migration has found its way into community traditions. Among the Tonga, whose male population is well over 50 percent migratory, a young boy's first migration is considered a sign of manhood.

Housing

The most common building materials in rural areas are wattle and daub (frameworks of rods and twigs packed with clay), specially grown bamboo, and thatch (cut grasses). Frequently, homes are round and windowless with thatched roofs and floors of packed earth. Most houses measure about 8 feet (2.4 m) in diameter.

Different ethnic groups have modified this basic design to suit their needs. The Yao first construct an outline of strong poles planted into the earth. They then cover this inner frame with another framework of hollow bamboo. The Ngoni design houses that taper upward at both ends—a shape that resembles a ship. Western and Arab influences, however, have changed building patterns in some areas. The Sena, for example, frequently put up rectangular houses with windows and paneled doors.

A woman sweeps the ground around her home in a Malawian village.

Rural buildings require constant upkeep. Within five to ten years, white ants will eat the bamboo supports and rain will crumble away the plaster. Furnishings for low-income rural dwellers are simple pieces made by local craftspeople. Wealthier rural inhabitants purchase deck chairs and rattan (cane) furniture.

The quality of urban housing depends on a person's income. It ranges from shanties (slums) to modern, Western-style accommodations. Most laborers who come to cities in search of work leave their families behind in rural villages because urban living is costly. Even for shantytown dwellers, water can cost several cents per day. A shanty with a corrugated (grooved) tin roof may rent for half of the average laborer's monthly salary.

In response to the population's move to the cities, the government pays to supply an area with roads, water, and outhouses. In return, renters build their own homes. Nevertheless, the spread of unhealthy shantytowns—and of the diseases such as cholera, dysentery, and malaria that flourish in them—continues.

◉ Health

Historically, Malawi's medical programs have focused on curing, rather than preventing, disease. In the early twenty-first century, however, disease prevention has become a priority. The Mutharika administration has made health a high priority. An increasingly larger portion of the nation's budget is spent on health improvements, especially in the areas of malaria and HIV/AIDS.

Malaria is a disease caused by parasites that live in mosquitoes. When a mosquito bites a person, the parasites enter the person's bloodstream. Consequently, the person may contract malaria. Malaria is marked by fever, chills, joint pain, vomiting, and convulsions. Left untreated, it can be fatal. Malaria is the second-highest cause of death among adults in Malawi. It is the number one killer of Malawian children. Every day in Malawi, 110 people die of malaria. Nearly half of them are under the age of eighteen.

HIV is the virus that causes the deadly disease

In an attempt to curb the spread of malaria, insecticide-treated bed nets are distributed at rural health clinics. When people cover their beds with these nets, they and their sleeping children are protected from disease-carrying mosquitoes. Relief organizations such as AmeriCares, Africare, Doctors Without Borders, and Oxfam America have distributed thousands of bed nets to Malawian mothers, whose children's lives have been saved from malaria.

41

ORPHANED BY AIDS

There are more than ten million AIDS orphans in Africa. AIDS orphans are children who have lost one or both of their parents to AIDS. In some cases, children themselves are infected with HIV/AIDS. In Malawi, there are one million AIDS orphans. They endure extreme poverty and hardship. Often, children as young as eight years old are caring for their younger brothers and sisters. Many AIDS orphans live in orphanages (places dedicated to the care of orphans). There they receive clothing, water, food, health care, and education. Community-based programs and international charities also provide for the children's needs. Volunteers in these programs and charities give the children love, comfort, and hope for the future.

Children orphaned by AIDS play at an orphanage in a village 30 miles (48 km) outside Lilongwe.

acquired immunodeficiency syndrome (AIDS). Malawi is one of the African countries hardest hit by HIV/AIDS. It accounts for 59 percent of deaths (or about 84,000 per year) among Malawians between the ages of fifteen and fifty-nine. Malawi's first AIDS case was reported in 1985. In response, the government created the National AIDS Control Programme (NACP) in 1988 to coordinate the country's AIDS education and HIV prevention efforts. The program did little to curb the disease. Another factor in the program's lack of success was the taboo nature of the subject: Malawians do not discuss sex openly. By 1993 HIV prevalence (rate of infection) among Malawian women had risen from 2 percent in the 1980s to 30 percent. In 2004 President Mutharika established the first National AIDS Policy. The policy, combined with aid from the U.S. government and the Global Fund to Fight AIDS, Tuberculosis, and Malaria, has provided a number of AIDS prevention and support programs. These include free drugs for those who are infected and increased testing for those who are not. The success of these efforts has stabilized the spread of HIV/AIDS, so that in the early 2000s, 14 percent of the entire population of Malawi suffers from HIV/AIDS. Several urban areas, such as Lilongwe, have witnessed a decline in HIV/AIDS cases, but some rural areas have seen an increase in cases.

A major portion of the country remains unsanitary and threatened by disease. The thatched roofs of houses support rats and insects that can spread disease. Livestock is often kept too close to wells, resulting in impure water. Most rural wells are checked once or twice a year by a mobile government mini laboratory, but this has proved inadequate. Not even urban residents are assured of safe drinking water.

Even in the cities, waterborne diseases can be a problem. During an outbreak of cholera in the city of Blantyre in 2002, more than one thousand people died. In 2008 water supplies in Blantyre were regularly cut off for as many as three days at a time. The city's water supplier announced the cuts would continue until 2013 as it replaces outdated water pumps with new ones.

Malawi's infant mortality rate is 96 per 1,000 live births in the early 2000s. Among African nations, only Mali (103 per 1,000) and Sierra Leone (156 per 1,000) recorded worse figures. Between 30 and 50 percent of all children born in Malawi die by the age of five. Nevertheless, new medical facilities have helped to lower the death rate, especially among young children. It is common to find families with four or five children, all of whom have survived to adulthood.

However, average life expectancy in Malawi is only forty years. As a result, 46 percent of the population is under fifteen years of age. Less than 3 percent are over sixty-five.

Visit www.vgsbooks.com for links to websites with additional information about efforts to improve health and life expectancy in Malawi.

◉ Education

More than 70 percent of Malawian boys and 49 percent of Malawian girls are enrolled in primary school. In 1994 primary school education was made free and compulsory (required). Generally, more children are enrolled than the schools can hold, so classes are often held outdoors. It is not unusual to see one teacher and as many as one hundred students in a class. Children start school when they are six years old. Primary school lasts eight years. Students must pass a test to go on to secondary school.

Students can attend government or private secondary schools. Secondary schools last four years. Students who seek skilled employment after graduation study technical and vocational subjects. Students must pass two more exams, one each at the end of the second and fourth years. After the fourth year, students either go on to college or university, or enter the workforce.

About 64 percent of Malawians are literate (able to read or write a basic sentence) in Chichewa and English. Fewer rural dwellers are literate in English, however. Government-sponsored programs aim to increase the literacy rate to 80 percent by 2015.

In addition to schools operated by missions, the British Voluntary Service Overseas and the U.S. Peace Corps supply many teachers for the fast-growing secondary schools. Higher education is provided at the University of Malawi, which has five specialized colleges. Students can also attend college at Mzuzu University, which opened in the Northern Region in 1997. Five technical schools are also in operation.

A class meets outdoors in central Malawi. Older students sit at desks, but all the students lack textbooks and other supplies necessary to help them learn.

A girl dances with her friends in a Malawian village.

Clothing

Malawians in urban areas dress in Western-style clothing—from jeans and T-shirts to suits and skirts. Western-style clothing—mostly donations from foreign relief agencies—is also common in rural areas. Women throughout the country typically wear skirts or sundresses that fall below the knee. Men most commonly wear cotton or khaki trousers or jeans and button-down shirts. Shorts generally are not considered modest clothing because they do not cover the knees. Usually only children wear shorts. Some adults wear shorts at home, but not in public.

Batik is white cloth that has been hand-decorated in colorful designs. Wax is used to block out portions where no color is desired. Batiks are made into skirts and shirts.

In rural areas, women wear an additional article of clothing called a *chitenje*. A chitenje (plural: *zitenje*) is a piece of fabric sold in 2-yard (1.8 m) portions that a woman wears over her clothing. This outer wraparound skirt has a variety of uses. It serves as an apron, a basket, a potholder, a baby carrier, or anything else the woman needs. Zitenje are generally brightly colored and bear a variety of designs. For special events, women in religious or other social groups buy zitenje in matching patterns.

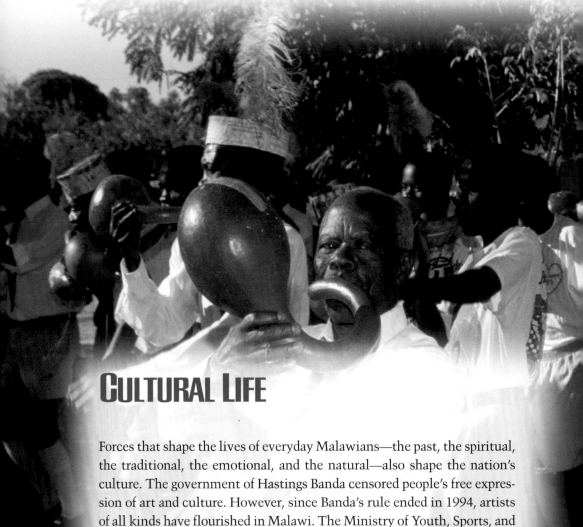

CULTURAL LIFE

Forces that shape the lives of everyday Malawians—the past, the spiritual, the traditional, the emotional, and the natural—also shape the nation's culture. The government of Hastings Banda censored people's free expression of art and culture. However, since Banda's rule ended in 1994, artists of all kinds have flourished in Malawi. The Ministry of Youth, Sports, and Culture works with local theater and cultural groups to connect artists and audiences from different social and economic classes. Their goal is to bridge ethnic and geographical differences to advance Malawian culture.

⊳ Literature

Malawians have a rich oral history. From ancient times to the present, they have passed stories, songs, and poems from one generation to the next through storytellers. The storytellers are sometimes accompanied by dancers.

Under President Banda, government control of the media in Malawi severely restricted the production of major works of contemporary lit-

erature. Aubrey Kachingwe's novel, *No Easy Task* (1966), explores the political struggles of a British colony moving toward independence. Legson Kayira's *The Detainee* (1972) is a tragic novel about an old man harassed by a youth brigade in an imaginary African country.

The Muluzi and Mutharika administrations loosened some of the rules against artistic expression. As a result, in recent years, the works of several Malawian poets—including David Rubadiri, Dalitso Baloyi, and Jack Mapanje—have drawn worldwide attention. In nonfiction, Mapanje has contributed to works about Malawi's political history. Elias C. Mandala has written many articles and books on the agrarian history of southern Malawi.

◉ Art

Malawi's different ethnic groups have a rich history of carving wooden items for royalty as well as for everyday use. Artists also make masks and other items for religious use.

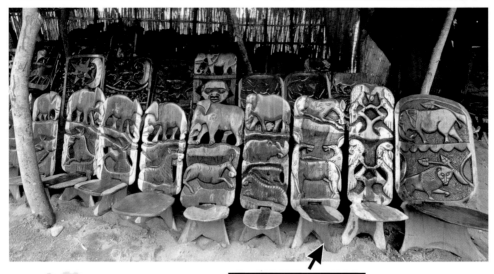

Elaborate carvings decorate these **Malawian chief's chairs.**

WISE WORDS

As in many African nations, proverbs are widely known and quoted in Malawi. Proverbs are sayings that convey advice, wisdom, or wit. The meanings of some of the most common Malawian proverbs, written in Chichewa, may be familiar:

Kabanga mwala—"The tortoise looks like a stone." (Things are not always what they appear.)

Chibanga mwala tsosenga nyala—"A rolling stone gathers no moss." (One who is always changing his or her mind will never get anything done.)

Mutu imodze tsosenga denga—"One head cannot support a roof." (Two heads are better than one.)

Malawian decorative objects are known for being intricately carved. Malawi's two best-known types of carvings are chief's chairs and three-legged tables.

Chief's chairs consist of two large pieces of mahogany or ebony wood. The largest piece serves as both the carved back of the chair and the front legs. The second piece fits through the lower section of the first and serves as the seat and the rear legs. The chairs are usually decorated with Malawian scenes, wildlife, dancers, or a combination of the three.

Three-legged tables reflect the skill of Malawian carvers. A round table is carved from mahogany or ebony. It is then decorated with carvings: a chessboard, a *bawo* (strategy game) board, or various African scenes. All three legs are carved from the same piece of wood, and the legs nest together in a sturdy, locked position. The tabletop can be removed and the three legs folded together for transport.

In tourist areas, merchants sell chief's chairs and three-legged tables. Stalls filled with ebony, mahogany, and teak wood carvings of Malawian scenes, masks, and ornaments line the streets.

Batiks are one of Malawi's most popular art forms. Malawian batiks are painted on white cloth, one color at a time. Wax is used to block out spaces where no color is desired. Malawian batiks represent specific scenes or individuals. Village life and nature are common themes. Batik fabric is made into skirts, shirts, tote bags, and purses.

Oil and acrylic painters work in Malawi as well. The most famous is David Kelly, who is internationally known for his oil paintings of nature scenes in Malawi. Kingsley Maigwa, another Malawian artist, donates his time teaching children in Mtendere orphaned by HIV/AIDS how to draw and paint.

Music and Dance

Modern music in Malawi incorporates many influences from foreign music. South African *kwela* is street music with jazz underpinnings. American rock and roll, soul, and funk also influence Malawi's music scene. *Kwasa kwasa*, a Malawian variety of Congolese dance music called soukous, and gospel music are also popular. Reggae has become immensely popular, especially along the shores of Lake Malawi where tourists gather. Lucius Banda, known by fans as the Soldier, is the best-selling reggae musician in Malawi. Other notable Malawian musicians are Joseph Tembo and Wambali Mkandawire. Malawian bands Tikhu Vibrations; Body, Mind & Soul; and the Black Missionaries have achieved international success. Traditional Malawian music uses rhythms from the Lomwe, Makuwa, and Nyanja peoples, and traditionalist performers such as Alan Namoko are known throughout the country.

Malawian musicians carefully craft their instruments. Most important are drums, which

MALAWI'S MUSIC FESTIVAL

Since 2004 the Lake of Stars music festival has taken place each autumn along the shores of Lake Malawi. The festival raises money for charity and promotes Malawian music. It also provides both tourists and Malawians the opportunity to experience live music performed by African and international artists. Performances range from African jazz to gospel. As well as the festival itself, Lake of Stars sponsors events all over the world to help fund the festival and raise awareness of Malawi's culture.

Musicians play on a beach at Cape Maclear in central Malawi. The boy in the center made his guitar from a discarded oil can.

musicians sometimes combine to form large drum orchestras. Instruments that accompany dancing are flutes, stringed instruments, and the *lipenga*, or singing horn—a wind instrument made from a specially treated gourd.

Like most African nations, Malawi has a rich dance tradition, which combines many individual ethnic ceremonies. Singing, playing, and rhythmic clapping accompany most dances. Although originally limited to certain ethnic groups, some dances have become known nationwide. *Gule wamkulu* (the big dance), for example, is a dance associated with a traditional religion of the same name. The dance was once connected to the crowning ceremonies of Chewa leaders. Parts of the dance also evolved from funeral dances. Performers wear masks and feathered headgear and cover themselves with mud, ash, or animal skins.

Religion

The majority of Malawians are Christian. Sixty percent of Christians are Protestant, and 15 percent are Roman Catholic. Other Christians include Baptists, Seventh-day Adventists, Anglicans, Church of

Central African Presbyterians (CCAP), and Jehovah's Witnesses. These Christian churches have established institutions throughout the country and contribute greatly in the fields of education and medical service.

Islam is also prominent in Malawi. Muslims (followers of Islam) make up about 20 percent of the population. Arab slave traders introduced Islam to Malawi in the early 1800s. The people of the Yao tribe, along the southern lakeshore, are most strongly associated with Islam. Almost every village in that region has a mosque (Islamic house of worship). Many women in the area wear veils that cover their heads, but not their faces, to follow the Muslim code of modesty. Some boys learn Arabic to pursue their study of the Quran (holy book of Islam).

Traditional beliefs also have a place in modern Malawian life and are practiced by about 5 percent of the population. Traditional religions revolve around the idea that all things—alive or dead, human or animal—are part of a vital life force. Deceased relatives and rulers are thought to watch over family and village affairs. Many Malawians combine Western Christian beliefs with traditional beliefs. For

President Banda did not approve of Jehovah's Witnesses, so he outlawed the religion in the 1980s. President Muluzi made it legal again in 1995. The religion has grown steadily since.

A **Muslim women's choir** performs religious songs in Blantyre.

A masked dancer performs the Gule Wamkulu dance at a Chewa funeral.

example, many Malawian Christians consult local African healers or participate in Gule Wamkulu. Gule Wamkulu is an animistic religion common among the Chewa people of the Central Region. (Animism involves spirit worship.)

Holidays

Malawians celebrate traditional Christian holidays such as Christmas and Easter, as well as a few nonreligious days that are uniquely British, including Boxing Day (December 26). In addition, Malawi has a few special holidays of its own—Chilembwe Day (January 15, which honors national hero John Chilembwe), Martyrs' Day (March 3, which honors those who gave their lives in Malawi's struggle for independence), and Kamuzu Day (May 14, which honors the birthday of Hastings Kamuzu Banda, Malawi's first president). Additional holidays are Labor Day (May 1), Freedom Day (June 14), Republic Day (July 6), August Holiday (August 6), and Mother's Day (October 17). Faithful Muslims observe the holy days of Islam. The most important is the daytime fast (time of not eating or drinking) during the Islamic holy month of Ramadan.

Sports and Recreation

Malawi's history as a British colony has influenced sports in the country. Football (soccer) is the most popular sport among schoolboys and

runs barefoot in an international athletic competition in Canada in 2001.

adult men. Malawi's men's national team competes in tournaments throughout Africa and in the biennial Africa Cup of Nations.

Netball, a game similar to basketball, is popular among schoolgirls. Malawi's women's team, called the Queens, is a member of the International Federation of Netball Associations. The team is highly ranked in international competition and has competed at the Netball World Championships.

In the late twentieth century, volleyball and basketball became popular sports among school-age Malawians. Cross-country running is also a fast-growing sport. Malawi's best-known long-distance runners are Catherine Chikwakwa, who trains in Germany, and Kondwani Chiwina, who represented his country in the 2004 Olympic Games in Athens, Greece. Other Malawian Olympians, also long-distance runners, are John Mwathiwa (1988, 1992, 1996) and Smartex Tambala (1992). In the 2000s, tennis and squash (an indoor sport similar to racquetball) are gaining a growing number of participants throughout the country.

Visit www.vgsbooks.com for links to websites with additional information about Malawi's best athletes. Listen to samples of music from Malawi, and look at examples of Malawian art.

Two **children play bawo** on a board dug out of the dirt.

The best-known game in Malawi is bawo. People all over Africa play bawo, and it is known as African chess. Variations of the game are called *mankala*, *oware*, and *coro*. Players move pebbles along cups in a board in an effort to capture their opponent's pebbles. The most common form of the game uses four rows of cups—two per opponent. Bawo games are highly competitive and may last from several hours to a day or two.

Food

The staple food in Malawi is *nsima*, a thick corn porridge. The porridge is molded into patties and served with either beans, meat, or vegetables in a tomato-and-onion sauce called *ndiwo*. Malawians also often eat cassavas (a starchy root) and potatoes. Rice is considered a luxury and saved for guests or special occasions.

Malawians consider food important to hospitality. They go out of their way to feed a guest, even if they have little to offer. Regardless of whether it is mealtime, the guest is served nsima or ndiwo. At mealtimes the guest is served first. Guests are encouraged to eat until they are full. In fact, custom dictates that guests be served so much food that they can't finish everything on their plates.

Although fish provides a major source of animal protein, many families cannot afford to eat it often. Like most Africans, Malawians eat local products such as fruits, vegetables, nuts, grains, meats, and eggs. A typical Malawian meal consists of *nkhuani relishe* (pumpkin leaves cooked with tomatoes and peanuts), *nyama pamodzi ndi mbatata* (meat stewed with tomatoes, onions, and potatoes), and *guava okazinga* (fried guavas, a pear-shaped fruit).

In most homes, food is cooked over a wood fire. Women (and children as helpers) are responsible for everything concerning the food, from growing it in backyard gardens, to shopping at outdoor markets, to cooking and cleaning up afterward.

Most villages have some kind of restaurant. The most common is the "chippie"—a metal stand used to fry potatoes over a fire. Customers either purchase a small bag to go or eat directly off the stand. Some villages have a mud-hut establishment that serves nsima or ndiwo at cheap prices. The major cities contain restaurants that serve Lebanese, Korean, Italian, or Indian food.

Malawians are fond of sugarcane, and it is common to see children walking along the road sucking on a piece of cane as if it were a stick of candy. Coffee and tea are commonly drunk at every meal. Beer is the national drink, but it is completely different from the brew known to people in Europe and North America. Malawian beer is so thick that it is more like a food than a beverage.

MBATATA (SWEET POTATO) COOKIES

Malawi is known as the "warm heart of Africa" due to the friendliness of the Malawian people. These cookies can be cut in heart shapes to commemorate Malawians.

¾ cup mashed sweet potato

¼ cup milk

4 tablespoons melted butter
  or margarine

1¼ cups sifted flour

2 teaspoons baking powder

2 tablespoons sugar

½ teaspoon salt

¼ teaspoon cinnamon

1. Preheat oven to 375 degrees.
2. Mix sweet potatoes, milk, and melted butter or margarine, and beat well.
3. Sift together the remaining dry ingredients and add to potato mixture. Mix well.
4. Turn dough onto a floured board, knead lightly, and roll out until dough is ½-inch (1.3 cm) thick.
5. Cut with a cookie cutter.
6. Place cookies on a greased baking sheet, and bake for 15 minutes or until cookies are light brown on the bottom.
7. Remove from baking sheet to cool. Sprinkle some extra cinnamon and sugar on top of the warm cookies.

THE ECONOMY

Tobacco, tea, sugar, peanuts, and cotton are Malawi's chief agricultural products and major exports (goods that are sold to foreign countries). Malawi's chief export partners include South Africa, Germany, Egypt, the United States, and Zimbabwe. Agriculture employs 90 percent of Malawians. The remaining 10 percent work in industry and services.

The economy depends heavily on financial aid from the International Monetary Fund (IMF), the World Bank, and donor nations, chiefly the United States and Great Britain. In 2006 Malawi was approved for relief under the Heavily Indebted Poor Countries (HIPC) program, a plan to relieve the debts of poor countries. In December 2007, the United States agreed to give large amounts of money to Malawi to improve its economy. Malawi must develop a five-year plan for economic growth before it receives the money. President Mutharika's government has begun a program with the IMF to reduce poverty and develop the economy. Other countries have offered aid as well.

◉ Services

The service sector includes jobs in and profits from education, government, health care, retail, trade, transportation, and tourism. Services average 45 percent of Malawi's gross domestic product (GDP—the amount of goods and services produced by a country in a year). Malawi has nine national parks and wildlife reserves that attract four hundred thousand visitors each year. Tourists add greatly to the economy of the country. Guided safaris (trips) into the parks and preserves offer activities that include hiking, birding, camping, horseback riding, and fishing. Malawians work as guides and drivers on safaris, as well as in tourist hotels and shops.

In the north, the 400-square-mile (1,000 sq. km) Vwasa Wildlife Reserve lies along the Zambian border northwest of Mzuzu. Elephants, hippos, three hundred species of birds, and many small mammals are found here. Nyika National Park is Malawi's largest park, with an area of 1,250 square miles (3,200 sq. km). Throughout the year, large herds of eland, zebras, roan, antelope, duikers, and reedbuck roam the grasslands.

Located on the western borders of the Central Region, Kasungu National Park covers 800 square miles (2,100 sq. km) of rolling savanna. Elephants and antelope are common, as are water buffalo and zebra. Leopards, hyenas, servals, and jackals can be seen too. Also in the Central Region is the Nkhotakota Wildlife Reserve, which is located near Lake Malawi and consists mostly of rugged terrain. Large animals on view include elephants.

In the far southwest is the 350-square-mile (900 sq. km) Lengwe National Park. Large numbers of nyalas—a rare species of antelope—roam freely in the region but are not found farther north in Africa. A 40-mile (64 km) circular drive with many branch roads enables visitors to see animals in their natural grazing areas and at their regular watering holes. Liwonde National Park is only 220 square miles (570 sq. km) but is Malawi's most popular park. Wildlife includes elephants, hippos, and crocodiles. Antelope include kudu, sable, and bushbuck.

Other parks and reserves in Malawi are Lake Malawi National Park, Majete Wildlife Reserve, and Mwabvi Wildlife Reserve. South Luangwa National Park in Zambia and Manda Wilderness Community Reserve in Mozambique are also accessed through Malawi.

Tourists watch for wild animals in Nyika National Park.

A **worker carries a bundle of tobacco leaves** out of a field. Once harvested, the leaves will be dried and packed into bales for export.

▶ Agriculture

Agriculture accounts for about 36 percent of Malawi's GDP. Malawian farmers have to cope with weather changes such as flooding and drought. Many attend government-sponsored farming courses.

Malawi ranks as a major exporter of various types of tobacco. About 50 million pounds (23 million kilograms) of the crop are exported yearly, much of it to Great Britain. Many small-scale farmers grow tobacco, particularly near Kasungu, in the Central Region.

Tea is the second-largest export crop. Much of it is grown in the Mlanje District. Started in 1878, the tea industry today employs thousands of Malawians to pick the more than 50,000 pounds (23,000 kg) of tea each year on plantations (large farms). Tea thrives on Malawi's high-altitude plateaus and hillsides.

Peanuts are grown for export crops and local food. Peanuts require a great deal of manual labor because they must be shelled and sorted by hand. Plant diseases have also been a problem. Nevertheless, peanuts are a good crop to rotate with corn and tobacco because they add nutrients to the soil.

Cotton grows mostly in the Southern Region, but it is also used as a rotation crop in the Central Region. The country also produces more than 50,000 tons (45,000 metric tons) of sugar a year, enough to meet its own needs and to sell the surplus to export partners.

Rice is grown in Malawi as a local food source. When more is grown than is needed, it is exported to nearby countries. Beans are a rotation crop rich in protein. Cassavas, macadamias, and citrus fruits are grown for local consumption but are also important export items.

Livestock production contributes about one-fifth of the value of total agricultural production. It consists mainly of subsistence grazing of sheep, cattle, goats, poultry, and pigs.

To meet the growing demand for timber and to lessen the need for importing it, the government began a forestry plan in the 1980s. Under this plan, 3,000 acres (1,200 hectares) are planted with trees each year, mostly on the plateaus and high mountain slopes. The government owns most of the timber plantations, although private industry has increased its involvement in the forestry business. The Imperial Tobacco Group grows eucalyptus trees to supply timber for its tobacco boxes and also makes plywood. The Forestry Department has planted thousands of acres of softwood trees.

Roughly one-fourth of Malawi's land area is forested. However, this includes a large amount of savanna woodland, which is only lightly forested. Woods are an important natural resource because they produce timber and protect the soil. Many small forests, mostly evergreen, thrive in the highlands and in the mountains. Some areas of the country support eucalyptus trees and pines.

TUNG OIL

Malawi is noted for its tea estates, but large estates of tung trees also grow in Malawi. Tung trees produce nuts that are processed to make tung oil. When applied to wood or other surfaces, tung oil provides a tough, waterproof finish. The oil is used to protect furniture and musical instruments such as guitars. It is also used as a finish for kitchen items such as wooden bowls and cutting boards. Tung oil seals granite or marble that will be used as countertops in kitchens and bathrooms.

Fish are the most important source of protein in the average Malawian's diet. The main fishing areas are Lake Chilwa, Lake Malombe, the southern end of Lake Malawi, and the lower reaches of the Shire River. Lake Malawi itself contains more than two hundred species of fish, many of them found nowhere else in the world.

Fishing techniques changed greatly in the late twentieth and early twenty-first centuries. Plank boats with outboard motors are used instead of dugout canoes with paddles. Fishing crews have adopted large-scale trawling methods. As a result, total catches have increased in the twenty-first century, rising from 70,000 tons (64,000 metric tons) in the 1980s to more than 90,000 tons (82,000 metric tons) in the 2000s.

A boy fishes with a net on Lake Malawi. Fishers keep what they need to eat and sell the rest of their catch to a processing plant.

Industry

In the twenty-first century, industry produces 19 percent of Malawi's GDP. This includes sawmill products, fish, cement, and consumer goods.

Separate timber plantations operate on the northern Viphya Plateau to provide raw material for the pulp and paper industries. A pulp mill near the railway at Salima (a central, lakeside district) enables Malawi to export wood pulp for packaging materials.

A fish cannery at Salima and a cold-storage plant at Mangochi process the catches for local sale. The most popular fish for canning are *chambo* and *nchila*, which resemble perch and carp, respectively. At least two hundred thousand Malawians make their living in the fishing industry, but problems with pollution and overfishing threaten to reduce yields.

Mining and Manufacturing

Mining for limestone, graphite, and granite is the major mining activity in Malawi. Limestone is the main ingredient in Malawi's thriving cement industry. Graphite and granite are building materials. Small deposits of gemstones such as agate, amethyst, aquamarine, garnets, rubies, and sapphires are also mined. Diamonds and rare metallic elements, such as lanthanum, are mined as well. A Malawian company has started an industry to produce gem-quality corundum. Corundum

This platinum mine operates on the shore of Lake Malawi.

is the raw material used to produce rubies and sapphires. Important bauxite deposits (the main source of aluminum) exist near Mlanje. However, the Malawian government has not expanded the mining industry to allow bauxite mining. Uranium, a raw material for producing nuclear energy, and asbestos exist in undetermined amounts.

The manufacturing industry exists to make products from the raw materials that are grown in Malawi. Immediately after independence, industrial development in Malawi was extremely rapid, with a growth rate of 17 percent per year. The increase of farm products—tea, tobacco, peanuts, rice, and sugar—that require processing has helped to speed up the growth of such processing industries. The making of pulp and paper has become an important industry.

Transportation

Malawi has four main transportation systems—road, rail, air, and water. Less than half of the 9,600 miles (15,450 km) of roads are paved, but they are constantly extended and improved. The road network already links Malawi with Mozambique, Zimbabwe, Zambia, and Tanzania. In addition, Malawi has railway access to Mozambique's Indian Ocean ports, its chief means of shipping exports to foreign markets.

Government-owned Air Malawi has regularly scheduled flights both within the country and to African nations such as Zimbabwe, Mozambique, Zambia, Kenya, and South Africa. Many other airlines have regular flights to and from the international airports near Blantyre and Lilongwe. A fleet of ships carrying both cargo and passengers operates on Lake Malawi. The fleet's headquarters at Monkey Bay features a dockyard and other facilities.

Transportation for the average rural dweller continues to mean walking. Cars and trucks are too expensive to own and to fuel with imported gasoline. Bicycles, though increasingly more common, are still considered luxuries. For those who live in the south—particularly along the shores of Lake Malawi—bus systems are relatively dependable and inexpensive. In general, inhabitants of the north travel without the convenience of modern transportation.

▶ Energy

Hydroelectric power has steadily replaced coal from Zimbabwe and oil from the Middle East as Malawi's chief source of energy for industry. While road transport still depends on imported fuel, more than 75 percent

A young man rides his bicycle down a road in **rural Malawi.**

of Malawi's electricity comes from water-driven turbines (engines). Gas-driven turbines supply the remaining 25 percent. Electricity consumption has grown at the rate of 20 percent a year and is controlled through a single public agency, the Electrical Supply Commission of Malawi.

In the early 2000s, alternative energy sources have included development of northern coal deposits. The production of ethanol fuel (grain alcohol made from crops such as corn and sugarcane) has increased every year since manufacturing began in 1982. Malawi currently produces 4.8 million gallons (18 million liters) of ethanol per year at its two ethanol factories.

◉ Communications and Media

About 103,000 telephone landlines are in use in Malawi, which is less than one for every one hundred people. Malawi Telecommunications, the country's phone company, was privatized (changed from government to private control) in 2006, bringing much-needed improvement to telecommunications services. There are nearly 500,000 cellular phones in use, but network coverage is limited and is based around the main urban areas.

Nine AM and five FM stations broadcast news, music, and information via radio to Malawians throughout the country. Two short-wave radio stations enable amateur radio broadcasters to interact directly with people inside and outside Malawi. Malawi's lone television broadcast station is operated by the government. There are 347 Internet hosts that bring access to nearly sixty thousand Internet users, most of whom live in or near the cities.

HUMAN DEVELOPMENT INDEX

The United Nations offers the Human Development Index (HDI) as a means to measure the well-being of the world's countries. The index measures life expectancy, literacy, standard of living, education, and GDP per person of 175 countries. The higher a country's rank, the more developed it is. The HDI in 2006 ranked Norway as number 1. Canada was number 6, and the United States ranked number 8. Malawi ranked number 162.

◉ The Future

Unlike most other nations on the African continent, Malawi has kept agriculture as the backbone of its economy rather than developing an industrial base. This strategy has made Malawi relatively self-sufficient in food production, but has slowed its growth in other economic areas.

Malawi's first president, Hastings Kamuzu Banda, ran a strict, one-party system for nearly

Women sort chili peppers at a large farm in Malawi.

thirty years after independence. Some of Banda's policies improved everyday life for Malawians. Other policies encouraged rural farmers to sell their crops instead of consuming them, which worsened the living standards of village populations. Subsequent presidents faced drought, food shortages, and government corruption. These challenges made it difficult to bring economic development to the country.

In the 2000s, Malawi's government operates under a multiparty system. The living standards of Malawians remain low, however. The majority of the rural population lives in poverty. Although government-sponsored health-care initiatives are slowly making gains, malaria and HIV/AIDS continue to ravage the population.

Malawi's future rests in disease education and prevention, as well as in job training and the promotion of tourism. Foreign businesses have begun to invest in Malawi. Malawians are working to create jobs and to establish their own businesses. They know their efforts will reduce poverty, instill self-confidence, and offer young people an opportunity to achieve economic success. Malawians are optimistic that the full potential of the warm heart of Africa will be achieved.

 Visit www.vgsbooks.com for links to websites with additional information about Malawi's economy, including facts about Malawi from the World Bank and the International Monetary Fund.

Timeline

CA. 100,000 B.C. Ancient peoples live in prehistoric Malawi.

CA. 3000 B.C. The Katanga and Kafula peoples live in the Lake Malawi region.

CA. A.D. 1 The Yao and other Bantu-speaking peoples move into northern Malawi from present-day Tanzania.

CA. 700S Arab slave traders arrive in present-day Malawi.

1480 The Maravi people establish the Maravi Empire.

1500S The Maravi easily absorb the Katanga. The Maravi fight the Kafula and drive them into present-day Zambia and Mozambique. Portuguese explorers are the first Europeans to arrive in what becomes Malawi.

1600S The Chewa and other Maravi peoples engage in long-distance trade with a coastal trading center in present-day Tanzania.

1800 Local Maravi leaders become independent of the larger Maravi Empire.

1817 Radama I signs an agreement to slow Madagascar's slave trade, which leads to the capture of many Maravi as slaves.

1835 Zwangendaba leads the Jere Ngoni into Malawi from southern Africa.

1858–1863 Scottish missionary and explorer David Livingstone maps the Shire River valley and Lake Malawi.

1860 The Maseko Ngoni move into the area of the Lilongwe Plain and Lake Malawi, blocking the movement of slave traders in the region.

1861 Livingstone establishes the first Christian mission in the Shire Plateau, making Malawi a center for missionary activity in central Africa.

1880S The Scramble for Africa begins. European countries compete to gain control of huge regions of Africa.

1882 Mandala House, Malawi's first two-story building, is erected in Blantyre. It is modern Malawi's oldest building.

1885 Missionaries at thirty-five Livingstonia missions teach trades, Christianity, and English to the people of Malawi without regard for their traditional ways of life.

1891 Great Britain establishes the Nyasaland Districts Protectorate.

1895 The British defeat Yao slave traders and occupy the southern part of Nyasaland. Johnston sets up a British-style government, making Zomba the capital.

1907 Colonial leaders rename the territory the Nyasaland Protectorate. Lawmaking councils, which exclude African members, are established.

1907   Colonial leaders rename the territory the Nyasaland Protectorate. Lawmaking councils, which exclude African members, are established.

1912   The first Native Association is established at Karonga. By the 1930s, nine other associations exist.

1915   John Chilembwe leads a small number of followers in a revolt against the British called the Chilembwe Rising.

1944   The Nyasaland African Congress (NAC) becomes the first colony-wide African political organization.

1953   Great Britain forms the Central African Federation, which includes Nyasaland.

1964   Nyasaland becomes the independent republic of Malawi on July 6. Hastings Kamuzu Banda becomes its first president.

1967   Banda is appointed president for life.

1975   Lilongwe replaces Zomba as Malawi's capital city.

1992   Malawians suffer the worst drought of the century and call for economic and government reforms.

1993   Malawians vote to end one-party rule in the country.

1994   Malawi becomes a multiparty democracy. In free elections, Banda is defeated by Bakili Muluzi, a former member of Banda's government and the founder of the United Democratic Front (UDF).

1997   Banda dies in South Africa.

1999   Muluzi is reelected president of Malawi.

2004   Bingu wa Mutharika is elected president in a disputed election. The Lake of Stars music festival debuts.

2005   Mutharika leaves the UDF and founds the Democratic Progressive Party (DPP). A hydroelectric dam above Kapichira Falls is completed, bringing energy to the cities of Blantyre and Limbe.

2006   Madonna and her husband, Guy Ritchie, begin adoption proceedings of thirteen-month-old David Banda. Malawi is approved for relief under the Heavily Indebted Poor Countries (HIPC) program.

2007   The United States agrees to give money to Malawi to improve its economy. Mutharika vows to seek reelection in 2009.

2008   Former president Muluzi is placed under house arrest following reports that he is plotting an overthrow of President Mutharika. Madonna's documentary on Malawi, *I Am Because We Are*, premieres at the Tribeca Film Festival in New York City.

COUNTRY NAME Republic of Malawi

AREA 45,747 square miles (118,485 sq. km)

MAIN LANDFORMS Great Rift Valley, Lilongwe Plain, Lower Shire Valley, Mlanje Mountains, Nyika Plateau, Upper Shire Valley, Shire Plateau, Viphya Plateau

HIGHEST POINT Mount Mlanje, 9,855 feet (3,000 m) above sea level

LOWEST POINT junction of the Shire River at the border with Mozambique, 125 feet (38 m) above sea level

MAJOR RIVERS South Rukuru, Dwangwa, Bua, Lilongwe, Shire

ANIMALS antelope, baboons, baboon spiders, bar-tailed trogons, buffalo, bushbabies, bushbuck, caterpillars, cheetahs, civets, cormorants, crocodiles, Denham's bustards, duikers, eland, elephants, fish eagles, grasshoppers, hamerkops, hartebeests, hippos, hooded cobras, hyenas, hyrax, jackals, kudu, leopards, lions, mpasa, nyalas, owls, porcupines, red-tailed francolins, reedbuck, roan, sable, servals, sparrows, straight horn spiders, tortoises, vervet monkeys, water moccasins, waterbuck, wattled cranes, weaverbirds, white ants (termites), wild pigs, zebras

CAPITAL CITY Lilongwe

OTHER MAJOR CITIES Blantyre, Limbe, Zomba

OFFICIAL LANGUAGES English and Chichewa

MONETARY UNIT Malawian kwacha (MWK). 100 tambala = 1MWK

MALAWIAN CURRENCY

Malawian currency comes in notes (paper money) of 5, 10, 20, 50, 100, 200, and 500 kwacha. The kwacha is divided into 100 tambala. Coins have a value of 1, 2, 5, 10, 20, 50 tambala, and 1, 5, and 10 kwacha. The fairly stable inflation rate of 7.5 percent keeps exchange rates steady. As of mid-2008, 100 Malawian kwachas equal 70 US cents. Coins and paper money carry images of animals, Lake Malawi, and heroes such as John Chilembwe *(right)*.

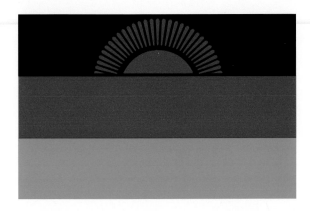

Malawi adopted a new flag when it became an independent country in 1964. The flag consists of three equal-sized horizontal stripes. The top stripe is black, the middle stripe is red, and the bottom stripe is green. A red, rising half-sun sits in the middle of the top black stripe. The rising sun represents the dawn of freedom and hope on the African continent. The black color represents the people of Africa. The red color represents the blood spilled by Malawians in their struggle for independence. The green color represents Malawi's vegetation.

Titled "Mulungu dalitsa Malawi" in Chichewa, Malawi adopted its national anthem in 1964. Michael-Fredrick Paul Sauka wrote the words and music. The English translation of the first two verses of "O God Bless Our Land of Malawi" is below:

O God bless our land of Malawi,
Keep it a land of peace.
Put down each and every enemy,
Hunger, disease, envy.
Join together all our hearts as one,
That we be free from fear.
Bless our leader, each and every one,
And Mother Malawi.

Our own Malawi, this land so fair,
Fertile and brave and free.
With its lakes, refreshing mountain air,
How greatly blest are we.
Hills and valleys, soil so rich and rare,
Give us a bounty free.
Wood and forest, plains so broad and fair,
All-beauteous Malawi.

For a link to a site where you can listen to Malawi's national anthem, "O God Bless Our Land of Malawi," visit www.vgsbooks.com.

HASTINGS KAMUZU BANDA (ca. 1906–1997) Born in Kasungu, he was educated in the United States and Scotland. After years of practicing medicine in both Great Britain and Ghana, he returned to Nyasaland in 1958 to lead the Malawi Congress Party (MCP). Banda was jailed by colonial leaders from March 1959 to April 1960. He became Malawi's first prime minister in 1963, and in 1966, he became Malawi's first president. Banda was named president for life in 1967 but was ousted in a 1994 election mandated by constitutional reform. He died in South Africa in 1997.

JOHN CHILEMBWE (ca. 1871–1915) Born in the Blantyre District of southern Malawi, John Chilembwe was a Baptist preacher who founded a school and served as a Christian missionary in the Blantyre area. In response to the treatment of Africans by European colonists, Chilembwe organized a rebellion at a cotton plantation near Blantyre in early 1915. Five people were killed in the short-lived uprising, which was quickly put down by British authorities. Many of the participants were executed. Others served long prison terms. Chilembwe tried to escape to Mozambique but was tracked down near the border and killed. The uprising was a forerunner of African nationalist movements.

STEVE CHIMOMBO (b. 1945) Born in Zomba, the old colonial capital, Chimombo is one of Malawi's best-known literary figures. He attended the Zomba Catholic Secondary School and was educated at the University of Malawi, as well as at universities in Great Britain and the United States. He is a poet, short-story writer, editor, literary critic, and professor of literature at the University of Malawi. His best-known work is *The Rainmaker*, a retelling of a hero story from the Chewa tribe.

DAVID KELLY (b. 1959) Born in Mlanje and educated in Rhodesia (present-day Zimbabwe), Kelly worked as a physical education teacher until 1983, when he decided to devote his career to art. He has since become world famous for his oil paintings of nature scenes in Malawi, as well as for three books he has written and illustrated about the natural beauty of Malawi. During the 1990s, Kelly ran a safari lodge in Liwonde, Malawi. In the 2000s, he lives in Scotland.

DAVIE LUHANGA (b. ca. 1983) Luhanga (known as Street Rat) is the lead singer of Body, Mind & Soul, a six-piece band from Mzuzu, in northern Malawi. The band started out playing reggae music but has created a musical concept called *voodjaz*, a mix of traditional Malawian rhythms and jazz. The band has won numerous national and international music awards and completed its first European tour in summer 2008. The band's goal is to bring Malawian culture to the rest of the world through their music.

JACK MAPANJE (b. 1944) Born in Kadango, Jack Mapanje is an internationally acclaimed poet, editor, and human rights activist. He was

Famous People

educated at the University of Malawi and the University of London. During the Banda regime, he was imprisoned for nearly four years without charge or trial because he was considered a radical. He is a lecturer at the University of Newcastle upon Tyne, in northeast England. His published works have earned a variety of prestigious awards and include *The Last of the Sweet Bananas: New and Selected Poems* (2004) and *Beasts of Nalunga* (2007).

BAKILI MULUZI (b. 1943) Born in Machinga, Muluzi was the second president of Malawi. He was educated in his home country and attended college in Europe. He returned to Malawi in the 1960s and joined Hastings Banda's Malawi Congress Party (MCP). In 1975 Muluzi was elected to the country's legislature, and he held a series of powerful government positions. In the early 1980s, Muluzi left government service. However, when the 1990s brought demands for reform in Banda's government, Muluzi formed a new political party called the United Democratic Front (UDF). In the first general election of Malawi's multiparty era, held on May 17, 1994, Muluzi defeated Banda. Muluzi served as Malawi's president until 2004.

BINGU WA MUTHARIKA (b. 1934) Born in Thyolo, Mutharika became president of Malawi in 2004 following a disputed election. Mutharika was educated in India and the United States and holds a PhD in development economics from Pacific Western University in California. During the 1970s, Mutharika was in the Malawi and Zambia civil services and joined the staff of the United Nations in 1978. He was appointed Malawi's minister of economic planning and development in 2002. He was nominated by President Bakili Muluzi to be the president's successor and won 36 percent of the popular vote in the 2004 election. In 2007 Mutharika announced that he would seek reelection in 2009.

DAVID RUBADIRI (b. 1930) Born in Liuli, David Rubadiri is a poet, playwright, university professor, diplomat, and permanent ambassador of his country to the United Nations. His works include *Growing Up with Poetry: An Anthology for Secondary Schools* (1989); *Poems from East Africa* (1971); *No Bride Price* (novel, 1967); and the play *Come to Tea* (1965). His work has appeared in international publications and story collections. He is an administrator at the University of Malawi.

SEODI VENEKAI-RUDO WHITE (b. ca. 1963) White is the national coordinator for Women and Law in Southern Africa Research and Educational Trust, a group that advocates for equal rights for women in Malawi. She speaks out in support of women's property rights, as well as employment opportunities equal to men and harsher penalties for men who are convicted of domestic violence. Her efforts have led to laws that allow widows to keep their property and the appointment of women to high government positions.

DEDZA Located 50 miles (80 km) southeast of Lilongwe, Dedza is the highest town in Malawi, with an altitude of 5,300 feet (1,600 m). The area has been settled since prehistoric times and old artistic traditions are still practiced. At Dedza Pottery, visitors can watch potters produce mugs, plates, table lamps, and tiles. Dedza Pottery products are found all over Malawi and are sold for export. In the hills around Dedza is the Chongoni Rock Art Area. Numerous natural shelters house ancient rock paintings that make up the densest cluster of rock art in central Africa. The area has been declared a World Heritage Site by the United Nations Educational, Scientific, and Cultural Organization (UNESCO).

LAKE MALAWI NATIONAL PARK Located at Cape Maclear, this is the world's first freshwater national park. It is also a UNESCO World Heritage Site. The park includes land around the cape and bay, as well as the lake and islands up to 330 feet (100 m) offshore. The park is like an aquarium of colorful tropical fish. Thousands of freshwater fish are more abundant here than anywhere else in the world. Boats take visitors on tour, and many fish feed directly from visitors' hands.

LILONGWE Lilongwe has been Malawi's capital since 1975 and is divided into two distinct cities within a city. Old Town has the appearance of a traditional Malawian settlement, including outdoor markets. Capital City consists of gleaming modern buildings, restaurants, luxury hotels, and a wide range of services. The State House is home to Malawi's National Assembly. Lilongwe Nature Sanctuary lies between Old Town and Capital City.

LIVINGSTONIA MISSION Dating to 1894 and located above Lake Malawi at 3,000 feet (900 m), Livingstonia Mission offers spectacular views across the lake to Tanzania. Buildings, including a church and the Old Stone House, offer a glimpse into mission life in Malawi before independence.

MANGOCHI Originally founded as Fort Johnston, Mangochi lies between Lakes Malawi and Malombe. The town consists of a number of historic monuments dating to the early 1900s, including a clock tower erected in memory of Britain's Queen Victoria, who ruled for much of the 1800s. There is also a museum and a modern Catholic cathedral.

THYOLO TEA ESTATES Between Blantyre and Mount Mlanje are the Thyolo Tea Estates. Tea has been grown here since 1908, and the entire area looks like a vast garden. Visitors can tour the estates and watch workers handpick tea leaves for sale and export. The nearby Thyolo Forest Reserve is a haven for hikers and bird-watchers.

animism: a religious practice of spirit worship. Spirit (conscious life) is believed to inhabit natural objects, natural events (such as storms and lightning), and human ancestors.

biennial: occurring every two years

caravans: groups of vehicles, wagons, or pack animals traveling together through a region

cholera: a disease caused by bacteria living in dirty water. Symptoms of cholera include diarrhea, nausea, vomiting, and cramps. People who don't receive medical treatment may die.

deforestation: the clearing of trees to make way for farmland or building construction

dictator: a leader who rules with absolute power, often through oppressive and violent means

dysentery: an infection of the digestive system that results in severe diarrhea. The major cause of dysentery is dirty water that contains microscopic organisms.

gross domestic product (GDP): the value of the goods and services produced by a country over a period of time, usually a year

impeach: to charge a public official with misconduct while in office

malaria: a disease caused by parasites that live in mosquitoes. Malaria is marked by fever, chills, joint pain, vomiting, and convulsions. Left untreated, malaria can be fatal.

propaganda: ideas, facts, or allegations spread deliberately to further a cause or to damage an opposing cause

protectorate: a region that signs a treaty to enter into a diplomatic relationship with a more powerful government. The more powerful government is called the protector. Protectors intend to provide military or diplomatic defense. Often, however, the result is exploitation of the protectorate's land, resources, and people.

rotation crop: a crop that is used in sequence with one or more other crops in the same plot of land. Rotation crops provide benefits such as avoiding the buildup of pests and the depletion of nutrients in the soil.

sleeping sickness: a disease common in tropical Africa that is marked by fever, headache, fatigue, confusion, and sleep disturbances and is caused by parasites that are transmitted by tsetse flies

Southern Hemisphere: the half of Earth that is south of the equator (the halfway point between the North Pole and the South Pole)

subsistence grazing: the feeding of livestock in which the animals have only enough food to survive, but not enough to be fattened for sale or slaughter as food

the West: the industrialized, non-Communist nations north and west of Africa, including the nations of Europe and the Americas

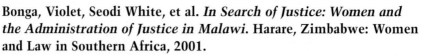

Bonga, Violet, Seodi White, et al. *In Search of Justice: Women and the Administration of Justice in Malawi.* **Harare, Zimbabwe: Women and Law in Southern Africa, 2001.**
This book reports the findings of a study on the challenges Malawian women face in accessing the country's justice system and explores a variety of solutions.

***Economist.* 2008.**
http://www.economist.com (May 16, 2008).
This weekly British magazine, available online or in print editions, provides excellent in-depth coverage of international news, including Malawi's economic and political news.

Else, David. *Malawi.* **Victoria, Australia: Lonely Planet, 2001.**
This useful guide features an illustrated section on Malawi's rich birdlife, information on traveling throughout the country, and more than twenty detailed maps.

Englund, Harri, ed. *A Democracy of Chameleons: Politics and Culture in the New Malawi.* **Uppsala, Sweden: Nordic Africa Institute, 2002.**
In this book, a variety of Malawian scholars explore the challenges Malawi has faced—and continues to struggle with—since independence, including poverty, hunger, equal justice under the law, HIV/AIDS, and women's rights.

Europa Publications. *Africa South of the Sahara 2008.* **London: Routledge, 2007.**
This annual guide focuses on the modern history and economy of Malawi and other southern African countries and includes statistics on population, health, agriculture, trade, education, and more.

Friends of Malawi. 2006.
http://www.friendsofmalawi.org (May 31, 2008).
Friends of Malawi was formed in 1987 by Peace Corps volunteers who had returned from Malawi. The organization's website contains a wealth of useful information about Malawian life and culture.

Mandala, Elias C. *The End of Chidyerano: A History of Food and Everyday Life in Malawi, 1860–2004.* **Chicago: Heinemann, 2005.**
In this work, Malawian author Mandala uses the history of southern Malawi to explain why famines do not occur more frequently in the region, despite chronic annual food shortages. Mandala also explores the daily and seasonal routines of agriculture in the area.

Meredith, Martin. *The Fate of Africa: A History of Fifty Years of Independence.* **New York: PublicAffairs, 2005.**
Meredith details the nationalist movements of Africa that began in the 1950s. When independence came to the countries of Africa, hopes were high that the continent's abundant natural resources and Western-educated leaders would combine to create stable, prosperous, democratic societies. Instead, violence, corruption, and political unrest marked the rule of many African leaders. Meredith explores solutions that may aid Africa's countries to fulfill their potential.

Morris, Brian. *The History and Conservation of Mammals in Malawi.* **Zomba, Malawi: Kachere Series, 2006.**
Using Malawi as a case study, this book is the first of its kind to be published in Malawi. It considers the role of animals in African human culture and history. The author examines the relationship between humans and mammals from prehistory to present day. He also explains how game parks and the protection of species came into existence and encourages Malawians to support mammal preservation.

Phillips, Henry. *From Obscurity to Bright Dawn: How Nyasaland Became Malawi, an Insider's Account.* **London: I. B. Taurus, 1998.**
This account, from a high-ranking British official in Nyasaland, tells the story of the country's transition from British colony to independent nation.

Population Reference Bureau. November 3, 2007.
http://www.prb.org (May 31, 2008).
PRB provides demographics on Malawi's population, health, environment, employment, and more.

2008 Country Profile and Guide to Malawi. **CD-ROM. New York: Progressive Management, 2007.**
This CD-ROM set contains more than one hundred thousand pages of information on Malawi—from climate and topography to the economy and transnational issues.

UNESCO World Heritage. May 17, 2008.
http://whc.unesco.org/en/list (May 31, 2008).
This site lists all the properties that UNESCO's World Heritage Committee "considers as having outstanding universal value," including two properties in Malawi. There is also a list of publications for more information, an explanation of UNESCO's World Heritage mission, and more.

U.S. Department of State, Bureau of African Affairs. *Background Notes: Southern Africa.* **Washington, DC: U.S. Government Printing Office, 2007.**
This is a brief overview of the statistics, people, history, government, economics, and foreign relations of the countries of southern Africa, including Malawi.

The World Factbook. October 9, 2007.
https://www.cia.gov/library/publications/the-world-factbook (May 31, 2008).
This site of the CIA (the U.S. Central Intelligence Agency) provides facts and figures on Malawian geography, government, economy, communications, transportation, and transnational issues.

Further Reading and Websites

Bawo: Simple Perplexity
http://bawo.zombasoft.com
If you want to learn how to play bawo, visit this site. It includes rules, answers to frequently asked questions, and links to related sites.

BBC News
http://news.bbc.co.uk/1/world/africa/country_profiles/1068913.stm
The World Edition of the BBC (British Broadcasting Corporation) News is updated throughout the day, every day. The BBC is a useful resource for up-to-date comprehensive coverage of Malawi.

Carter, Judy. *Malawi Wildlife, Parks and Preserves*. New York: Macmillan, 1997.
Though Malawi has preserved additional land areas since the publication of this book, this is a good introduction to Malawi's wilderness areas.

Conroy, Anne C., ed. *Poverty, AIDS and Hunger: Breaking the Poverty Trap in Malawi*. New York: Palgrave Macmillan, 2007.
The authors of this book argue that the cycle of poverty that surrounds Africa's poor people can be broken through a series of creative approaches, at a relatively low monetary cost. They use the example of Malawi to illustrate the challenges that poverty creates and the opportunities for change that exist.

Dedza Pottery
http://www.dedzapottery.com
Visit this site to learn more about Dedza pottery and see examples of its world-famous products.

Fuller, Alexandra. *Don't Lets Go to the Dogs Tonight: An African Childhood*. New York: Random House, 2001.
The author, the daughter of British settlers in Africa, recounts her childhood during the tumultuous years when countries on the continent were rebelling against British rule. The author details the family's moves to several African countries, including Malawi.

I Am Because We Are
http://www.iambecauseweare.com
At this site, you can find information on and a trailer for the film *I Am Because We Are*, which was written, produced, and narrated by Madonna. The documentary premiered at the Tribeca Film Festival in 2008. It chronicles the plight of Malawi's poverty-stricken people and may be released on DVD.

Lwanda, John Lloyd. *Kamuzu Banda of Malawi: A Study in Promise, Power, and Paralysis (1961 to 1993)*. Glasgow, UK: Dudu Nsomba Publications, 1993.
This book is both a biography of the late Malawian president and an in-depth study of the impact of his dictatorship on Malawi and its people.

Malawi Page
http://www.africa.upenn.edu/Country_Specific/Malawi.html
This site offers links to a wide range of sites featuring Malawi's languages, stamps and money, embassies, and newspapers. The African Studies Center is committed "to an interdisciplinary approach to the study of African people, their institutions, and the wider world where they now reside."

Mapanje, Jack. *The Last of the Sweet Bananas: New and Selected Poems*. Northumberland, UK: Bloodaxe Books, 2004.
This poetry collection features some of Mapanje's previously published works, as well as newer poems. It is a useful introduction to his themes, including human dignity and African liberation.

Pachai, Bridglal. *Malawi: The History of a Nation*. Essex, UK: Longman, 1973.
This book is a useful resource for understanding the early history of the region that became Malawi.

Sierra, Judy. *The Mean Hyena: A Folktale from Malawi*. Boston: Dutton, 1997.
Fisi the hyena learns an important lesson when he plays a trick on Kamba the tortoise.

vgsbooks.com
http://www.vgsbooks.com
Visit vgsbooks.com, the home page of the Visual Geography Series®. You can get linked to all sorts of useful online information, including geographical, historical, demographic, cultural, and economic websites. The vgsbooks.com site is a great source for late-breaking news and statistics.

Index

AIDS, 7, 36, 41–43, 65; orphans and, 42, 49
animals, 15, 16–18, 41, 57–58, 60, 72
animism, 24, 50, 51–52
arts and crafts, 20, 46, 47–49, 50, 70, 72, 80; rock art, 20, 72, 80

Baloyi, Dalitso, 47
Banda, Hastings Kamuzu, 5, 31–33, 37, 46, 51, 52, 64–65, 70
Banda, Lucius (the Soldier), 49
Bantu, 20, 39
baobab trees, 16
batik, 45, 49
bawo (game), 48, 54
Booth, Joseph, 28, 29

Cape Maclear, 50, 72
cars, 63
censorship, 33, 46
Central African Federation, 29–30
Chikwakwa, Catherine, 53
Chilembwe, John, 28–29, 31, 52, 68, 70
Chilembwe Rising, 29, 70
Chimombo, Steve, 70
Chipembere, Henry, 30
Chiume, Kanyama, 30
Chiwina, Kondwani, 53
Chongoni Rock Art Area, 20, 72, 80
cities, 18–19, 36, 72, 80; Blantyre, 13, 18, 19, 36, 80; Dedza, 20, 72, 80; Lilongwe, 19; Zomba, 19, 36
civil and human rights, 33, 71
climate, 15–16, 19, 59
clothing, 7, 33, 45, 49, 51
corruption, government, 4, 7, 32–33, 34, 65

dams, 13
Dedza, 20, 72, 80
deforestation, 18
drought, 5, 18, 33, 34, 59

economy, 5, 7, 13, 19, 56–65; agriculture, 13, 56, 59–60, 62, 64–65; communications, 64; energy, 13, 63–64; industry and manufacturing, 61–62; migratory workers, 38, 39–40; mining, 7, 13, 33, 34, 39, 61–62, 64; services,

57–58; tourism, 14, 49, 57–58, 72; trade, 56, 59; transportation, 62–63
education, 7, 19, 24, 29, 33, 43–44
Elephant Marsh, 14
energy and electricity, 13, 63–64
environmental issues, 17–18, 61
equator, 15
ethnic groups, 5, 20–21, 26, 29, 30, 37–40, 47, 49; Chewa, 5, 22, 23, 37; Maravi, 5, 21–23, 37; Nyanja, 5, 37, 38, 49; Yao, 20, 23, 24, 25, 27–28, 38, 40, 51

family, 39–40, 41
farms and farming, 11, 16, 30, 56, 59–60, 64–65, 72, 80
films, 34
fish and fishing, 17, 60–61, 72
food, 34, 54–55, 59, 60, 64; recipe, 55
foreign aid and relations, 7, 19, 41, 44, 45, 56
forests, 16, 18, 60, 61

Great Britain, 4, 22, 24–25, 31, 56
Great Rift Valley, 8–9
gross domestic product (GDP), 57, 59, 61

health, 7, 17, 18, 41–43, 65
Heavily Indebted Poor Countries, 56
history, 4–5, 7, 20–35; ancient era, 4, 20–21; Banda era, 31–33, 70, 71; British rule, 4, 19, 22, 26–32, 39, 52; Christian missions, 23–26, 28; independence, 4–5, 32; Maravi Empire, 21–23; nationalism, 29–31, 70; resistance to British rule, 28–29
holidays and festivals, 52, 80
housing, 18, 19, 40–41
Human Development Index (HDI), 64
hydroelectricity, 13, 63–64

Internet, 64
Islam, 51, 52

Johnston, Harry, 27

Kachingwe, Aubrey, 47
Kamwendo, Rodwell, 53
Kayira, Legson, 47

Kelly, David, 49, 70

Lake Malawi National Park, 58, 72
lakes, 13–14, 15; Malawi, 4, 9, 14,
    15, 24, 49, 58, 63, 73
landscape, 4, 8–9, 11–15
languages, 20, 25, 28, 33, 37, 38, 39,
    44; official, 39
life expectancy, 43
lifestyles, 5, 18, 19, 41, 43, 45, 54–55,
    65, 80; migratory, 38, 39–40, 41
literacy rate, 44
literature, 46–47, 48, 70–71
Livingstone, David, 24
Livingstonia Mission, 25, 72
Luhanga, Davie, 70

Madonna, 7, 34
Maigwa, Kingsley, 49
Makanjira, 28
malaria, 41
Malawi: anthem, 69; boundaries,
    size, and location, 4, 8; climate,
    15–16, 19, 59; currency, 68; flag,
    69; flora and fauna, 16–18, 57–58,
    72; government, 34–35; maps, 6,
    10; name of, 4–5; population, 7, 11,
    18, 36; topography, 4, 8–9, 11–15
Mangochi (Fort Johnston), 27–28, 72
Mapanje, Jack, 70–71
Maravi Empire, 21–23
minerals and mining, 7, 13, 33, 34,
    39, 61–62, 64
missions and missionaries, 23–26, 28
mountains, 8, 12, 15, 80
Mount Mlanje, 12, 80
Mozambique, 8, 9, 15, 22, 34, 36, 38,
    58, 62
Muluzi, Bakili, 7, 33–34, 71
music and dance, 46, 49–50, 70, 80
Mutharika, Bingu wa, 7, 34, 41, 56, 71
Mwathiwa, John, 53

names, 5, 39
national parks, 17–18, 57–58, 72
natural resources, 4, 13
Nyasaland, 4, 27–32
Nyasaland African Congress (NAC),
    29, 30–32
Nyika Plateau, 11–12, 80

political parties, 29–31, 33, 34, 70, 71
pollution, 18, 43, 61
poverty, 4, 7, 42, 56, 65
protectorate, 4, 27–32
proverbs, 48

Radama I, 23
railways, 26
rainfall, 16. See also drought
recipe, 59
religions, 24, 29, 50–52; Christianity,
    24, 50–51, 52, 70; Islam, 51, 52;
    traditional African, 24, 50, 51–52
rivers, 13, 14–15, 26
roads, 7, 33, 41, 62, 63
Rubadiri, David, 47, 71
runners, 53

safaris, 57, 58
sanitation, 18, 41, 43
Scramble for Africa, 26–27
Shaka, 23
slave trade, 4, 21, 22, 23, 24, 25, 26,
    27, 51
sports and recreation, 52–54

telephones, 64
television, 64
temperatures, 15–16, 19
Thyolo Tea Estates, 72
tourism, 14, 49, 57–58, 72
transportation, 7, 18, 26, 33, 62–63
tung oil, 60

UNESCO World Heritage Sites, 72
United Nations (UN), 64, 71
United States, 56, 64

water, 18, 41, 43
White, Seodi V., 71
women, 7, 33, 35, 36, 45, 51, 53,
    55, 71
workers, migratory, 38, 39–40
World Bank and IMF, 56

Zambia, 8, 22, 27, 36
Zulus, 23

Captions for photos appearing on cover and chapter openers:

Cover: Women carry buckets of water home from a well in Malawi.

pp. 4–5 Mount Mlanje rises above tea plantations in southern Malawi.

pp. 8–9 Flowers cover a meadow on Malawi's Nyika Plateau.

pp. 36–37 A street vendor displays rugs for sale in the city of Blantyre.

pp. 46–47 Villagers dance and play lipengas, wind instruments made from gourds, during a festival on Likoma Island in Lake Malawi.

pp. 56–57 Women tend a community field in a village outside of Liwonde in southern Malawi.

Photo Acknowledgments

The images in this book are used with the permission of: © Jon Spaull/Axiom Photographic Agency/Getty Images, p. 4–5; © XNR Productions, pp. 6, 10; © age fotostock/SuperStock, p. 8–9; © Bill Curtsinger/National Geographic/ Getty Images, p. 11; © Lynda Huxley/Images of Africa Photobank/Alamy, p. 12; © Ariadne Van Zandbergen/Alamy, pp. 13, 14, 15, 36–37, 46–47, 58; © John Warburton-Lee/Danita Delimont/drr.net, p. 16; © Larry Dale Gordon/ Photographer's Choice/Getty Images, p. 17 (left); © Jason Gallier/Alamy, p. 17 (right); © Lynda Huxley/Alamy, p. 19; © Mary Evans Picture Library/Alamy, pp. 23, 25, 26; Library of Congress (LC-USZ62-16529), p. 24; © UPPA/NHPA/ Photoshot, p. 27; © Bert Hardy/Stringer/Getty Images, p. 30; © Terrence Spencer/ Time Life Pictures/Getty Images, p. 31; © Joe Alexander/AFP/Getty Images, p. 34; © Michael Harder/Alamy, p. 35; © Per-Anders Pettersson /Getty Images, pp. 38, 42; © Jan Banning/Panos Pictures, p. 40; © Frank May/dpa/CORBIS, p. 44; © Penny Tweedie/Stone/Getty Images, p. 45; © Cathy Lanz/africanpictures. net/The Image Works, p. 48; © Neil Cooper/Panos Pictures, p. 50; © Ira Lippke/ ZUMA Press, p. 51; © Images & Stories/Alamy, pp. 52, 61; © Andy Lyons/ ALLSPORT/Getty Images, p. 53; © Giacomo Pirozzi/Panos Pictures, pp. 54, 59; Per-Anders Petterson/Reportage/Getty Images, 56–57; © Jack Barker/Alamy, p. 62; © Patrick Brown/Panos Pictures, p. 63; © Karin Duthie/africanpictures.net / The Image Works, p. 65; Audrius Tomonis—www.banknotes.com, p. 68; © Laura Westlund/Independent Picture Service, p. 69.

Front cover: © Mikkel Ostergaard/Panos Pictures. Back cover: NASA.